Albatros Aircraft of WWI
Volume 3: Bombers, Seaplanes, J-Types
A Centennial Perspective on Great War Airplanes

Jack Her

Great War Aviation Centennial Series #26

This book is dedicated to exceptional historian and kind, generous, and humorous gentleman Michael Schmeelke.

Acknowledgements

My sincere thanks to Reinhard Zankl for his insightful information and comments about production orders and serial numbers and for photographs, to Colin Owers for information, photographs, and scale drawings, and Greg VanWyngarden, Bruno Schmäling, and Boris Ciglic for photographs. Thanks also to Bob Pearson for his color profiles, Aaron Weaver for feedback, digital photo editing, and cover design, Martin Digmayer for scale drawings, Jim Miller for the colorized photograph used for the cover, and the Deutsches Technikmuseum in Berlin and The Museum of Flight in Seattle for photographs. Any errors are my responsibility.

Color aircraft profiles © Bob Pearson. Purchase his CD of WWI aircraft profiles for $50 US/Canadian, 40 €, or £30, airmail postage included, via Paypal to Bob at: bpearson@kaien.net

For our aviation books in print and electronic format, please see our website at: www.aeronautbooks.com. I am looking for photographs of the less well-known German aircraft of WWI for future titles. For questions or to help with photographs please contact me at jherris@me.com

Interested in WWI aviation? Join The League of WWI Aviation Historians (www.overthefront.com) and Cross & Cockade International (www.crossandcockade.com).

ISBN: 978-1-935881-49-0

© 2017 Aeronaut Books, all rights reserved
Text © 2017 Jack Herris
Design and layout: Jack Herris
Cover design: Aaron Weaver
Digital photo editing: Aaron Weaver & Jack Herris

www.aeronautbooks.com

Table of Contents

Albatros Bombers, Seaplanes, J-Types	3
Albatros J-Types	4
Albatros J.I	6
Albatros J.II	33
Albatros Bombers	44
Albatros G.I	44
Albatros G.II	46
Albatros G.III	50
Albatros Seaplanes	64
Albatros WDD & W.1	66
Albatros W.2	82
Albatros W.3	84
Albatros W.4	90
Albatros W.5	106
Albatros W.8	112
Albatros Miscellaneous L-Types	115
Albatros L3	115
Albatros L9	116
Albatros J-Types, Bombers, and Seaplanes In Retrospect	118
Bibliography	119
Index	119
Scale Drawings	
Albatros J.I	120
Albatros J.II	124
Albatros G.III	128
Albatros W.4 (early)	131
Albatros W.4 (late)	134
Albatros W.5	137
Afterword	140

Foreword

This is the third of four volumes covering all Albatros aircraft of WWI; the fourth focuses on the many Albatros fighter designs.

In addition to reconnaissance planes and fighters, Albatros was one of three manufacturers to produce operational armored warplanes for Germany. The Albatros J-types form the first part of this book.

Albatros designed and built three bomber designs, with the G.III being produced in small numbers and used at the front. The Albatros bombers are the middle section of this book.

Finally, Albatros produced a number of seaplanes; these are covered in the final section of this book.

Jack Herris

Below: The sole Albatros G.II prototype under test at Johannisthal. An Albatros C.V is in the background. (Peter M. Grosz Collection/SDTB)

Albatros Bombers, Seaplanes, J-Types

When Albatros responded to *Idflieg's* requirement for an armored infantry aircraft, the resulting J.I was based on the C.XII's wood airframe. To save weight, the engine was left without armor, the only J-type lacking that vital attribute. The competing Junkers and AEG J-types had metal airframes and armored engines, making them far less vulnerable to ground fire. After aircrew complaints, the follow-on Albatros J.II added engine armor. However, the J.II retained the wood airframe of the J.I. As a result, Albatros J-types were built in only limited numbers despite Albatros's huge production capacity. The AEG and Junkers J-types were both produced in greater numbers even though they were harder to build.

It was only natural that Albatros would try its hand designing bombers as well as other types. Both the four-engine G.I and two-engine G.II remained single prototypes. However, the two-engine G.III, developed from the G.II prototype, was produced in small numbers and used in combat. Nonetheless, the competing Gotha, AEG, and Friedrichshafen bombers all proved superior and Albatros exited bomber design and manufacture.

Albatros had experimented with seaplanes before the war started and early in the war built a variety of unarmed, single-engine, two-seat floatplanes for reconnaissance and training. Most of these aircraft were the WDD and its W.1 development. However, the Friedrichshafen FF33 series proved more robust in operational service and Albatros seaplane production remained comparatively minor. Albatros also developed the W.3 two-engine torpedo seaplane; a handful of its W.5 development was built.

By far the most successful Albatros seaplane was its W.4 single-seat fighter, which was a floatplane development of the successful Albatros D.I fighter used by the Army. The W.4 was one of the two most successful aircraft of its type; however, the Navy soon realized that a two-seat floatplane fighter offered significant advantages in combat and the W.4 and its single-seat companion types were relegated to pilot training. The Albatros W.8 two-seat fighter floatplane was not placed in production.

The Albatros J-Types

Above: Albatros J.I J.401/17, the second production aircraft, is shown at Adlershof undergoing evaluation. The nose has a spinner and streamlined shape because there was no armor around the engine. The Albatros J.I was the only J-type without engine armor and was therefore the aircraft most vulnerable to ground-fire of all the J-types.

Albatros was one of three manufacturers that responded to Idflieg's requirement for an armored infantry contact aircraft with their J.I and later J.II. Significantly, the large Albatros firm produced the fewest J-types; moreover, they were the last to reach the front. Given the huge production capacity of Albatros, this is a strong indication that the competing Junkers and AEG J-types were superior to the Albatros J-types. Certainly the Albatros J.I, with its exposed radiator and no engine armor, was the J-type most vulnerable to ground fire, and thus the least successful. Although the Albatros J.II rectified those weaknesses, the wood structure of the Albatros J-types made them more vulnerable to ground fire than the metal Junkers and AEG designs; therefore they were produced in the smallest numbers despite Albatros's production capacity.

Despite its installation in all operational J-types, the Benz B.IV/IVa of 200/220 hp was clearly insufficient for these heavy aircraft. For example, the Albatros J.I was developed from the C.XII and its armor meant it was more than 800 pounds (almost 400 kg) heavier, yet the 260 hp Mercedes in the C.XII was replaced with a 200 hp Benz! Thus the J-types were significantly underpowered even by the modest standards of the time, resulting in long take-off runs, thereby reducing the number of airfields that could be used. Their low power also resulted in low speed, which, together with their higher stall speed due to their heavy armor, provided a relatively small maneuvering speed margin above the stall compared to their unarmored contemporaries. This reduction in their flight envelope made them less forgiving to fly and reduced their safety margin during normal flight operations. Being underpowered also reduced their agility and made them more vulnerable to fighters. Aware of aircrew criticism, in April 1918 *Idflieg* suggested use of the more powerful 260 hp Mercedes D.IVa engine in J-type aircraft to improve their ability to operate from small fields. Because the Mercedes D.IVa engine was not an over-compressed, high-altitude design, it was suitable for the low-flying J-types, but this upgrade was never implemented during the war.

Above & Below: Albatros J.I J.415/17 with factory finish and *Flieger-Abteilung (A)* 238 unit markings. The early J.I aircraft used the wing and tailplane camouflage of the late Albatros C-types like the C.XII together with varnished wood rear fuselage and light-gray armor. Over this J.415/17 has black and white elevator stripes, white stripes over the upper wing, and a white field on the upper fuselage behind the gunner with a Roman numeral painted on it, in this case 'VI', which were the *Flieger-Abteilung (A)* 238 unit markings. The closeup view shows the armored door to the pilot's cockpit open.

Albatros J.I

Above: Albatros J.I J.401/17 at Adlershof. The J.I used the wings and tail of the Albatros C.XII fitted to its armored fuselage. The fuselage behind the armor was wood like the Albatros C-types. The wireless antenna lead is hanging below the observer's cockpit.

Below: An early production Albatros J.I, perhaps J.401/17, showing the propeller spinner used on the early machines.

The initial Albatros armored design, the Albatros J.I used the same basic wood wings and tail surfaces as the preceding Albatros C.XII reconnaissance plane. These readily-available components were coupled with a new engine and forward fuselage featuring 5 mm steel sheet armor around the crew cockpits. To maintain center of gravity with the lighter engine, the wings were given 2° of sweepback. In contrast to the airfoil radiator of the Albatros C.XII, the J.I had a box radiator installed in front of the leading edge of the upper wing. To limit weight, the J.I engine cowling and radiator were left unarmored; this led to frequent engine failures due to damage from ground fire.

Like all production J-types, the Albatros J.I used the Benz Bz.IV engine. This 200 hp engine was substantially less powerful than the 260 hp Mercedes D.IVa used in the C.XII from which the J.I was derived. The reduced power, coupled with the increased weight of the armor and increased drag,

Above: Albatros J.I J.424/17 after a bad landing. It carries a dark, probably black, zig-zag marking on the rear fuselage and a stylized tactical number '7'.

Albatros J-Type Specifications

	Albatros J.I	Albatros J.II
Engine	200 hp Benz Bz.IV	220 hp Benz Bz.IVa
Span, Upper	14.14m	14.1m
Span, Lower	13.45m	13.45m
Chord, Upper	1.70m	1.70m
Length	8.83m	8.44m
Track	2.0m	2.0m
Wing Sweepback	2°	1.5°
Wing Area	42.82 m^2	43.2 m^2
Empty Weight	1,398 kg.	1,515 kg.
Loaded Weight	1,808 kg.	1,927 kg.
Maximum Speed	140 km/h	140 km/h
Climb to 1,000m	11.2 minutes	11.2 minutes
Flight Duration	2.5 hours	2.5 hours
Armament	1 flexible machine gun, some aircraft 2 fixed machine guns	1 flexible machine gun, 2 fixed machine guns
Optional	20mm Becker Cannon	20mm Becker Cannon

significantly reduced J.I performance and agility compared to its reconnaissance aircraft predecessors. Initially the Albatros J.I had a very streamlined nose complete with propeller spinner, but this was soon found to be unnecessary for such a slow aircraft and later production aircraft replaced the spinner with a rounded nose, which actually reduced drag.

Initially, the armament consisted of one flexible Parabellum MG14/17 for the observer. Later, some aircraft were equipped with two LMG 08/15 machine guns fixed in the fuselage floor, which could fire diagonally forward and down at a 45°

Albatros J-Type Production Orders

Serial Numbers	Qty	Type and Order Date	Lowest Known Serial	Highest Known Serial
1917 Serials				
J.400–424/17	25	Albatros J.I	J.400/17	J.424/17
J.700–774/17	75	Albatros J.I	J.701/17	J.758/17
1917 Subtotal	100			
1918 Serials				
J.100–124/18	25	Albatros J.I	J.101/18	—
J.125–174/18	50	Albatros J.II ordered Feb. 1918	J.126/18	J169/18
J.616–715/18	100	Albatros J.II	J.616/18	J.714/18
1918 Subtotal	175			

- 125 Albatros J.I were ordered and delivered.
- 150 Albatros J.II were ordered and most, perhaps all, were delivered.

Above: Albatros J.I J.421/17 serving with *FA(A)* 293; the older style iron cross has been removed and the new style straight cross painted forward. The spinner and painted upper wing camouflage are first production batch features.

Above: Albatros J.I J.400/17 was sold to Austria-Hungary and became 09.01. Here it is ready for transport and may be on its way to Austria because the spinner has been removed and 09.01 had no spinner.

> ### Albatros J.1 Production Batches
> Albatros J.I production orders totaled 125 aircraft in three batches. Review of available photographs appears to show these characteristics:
> **First Batch of 25, serials J.400–424/17:**
> Spinners, painted camouflage on top of wings and tail surfaces (like the Albatros C.XII).
> **Second Batch of 75, serials J.700–774/17:**
> No spinners, painted camouflage on top of wings and tail surfaces (like the Albatros C.XII).
> **Third Batch of 25, serials J.100–124/18:**
> No spinners, printed camouflage fabric on all flying surfaces. Some had patterned camouflage on fuselage.
> **Note:** All Albatros J.II aircraft were apparently finished like late-production J.I aircraft.

angle. Furthermore, the crews carried light bombs and grenades, which were thrown by hand to attack troops and other ground targets.

The Albatros J.I was the first German aircraft that deployed a cannon in unrestricted operational service, as distinct from operational trials. In November 1917 the first tests began with the 20 mm Becker cannon, which was installed on the left side of the observer's cockpit of Albatros J.I J.710/17.

After firing 600 rounds in ground tests with the machine's rear fuselage elevated, in-flight firing tests began from the Albatros on 12 December 1917. It was shown that the recoil of the cannon proved substantially less than during the ground tests. Moreover, installation of the cannon hardly affected the in-flight handling characteristics. Target acquisition was deemed good, but the ammunition

Above: Albatros J.I J.402/17, the third production aircraft, is shown after a bad landing in December 1917. The J.I used the wings and tail surfaces of the C.XII but the fuselage was far less elegant. Early aircraft had a propeller spinner; that was soon abandoned as unnecessary for such a slow aircraft.

clip proved difficult to change in the slipstream. By the end of January 1918 testing was successfully completed with the exception of the clip-loading problem. In February this appeared to be solved by provision of a special handgrip on the ammunition clip. Three cannon-armed J.I aircraft were then sent to the front, primarily intended for tank busting, followed by five more in April. Each of these machines had a captured Lewis machine gun installed in the observer's cockpit for defense against fighters; the Lewis was used to save weight.

These eight cannon aircraft underwent combat evaluation with *Schlachtstaffeln* 10, 17, and 28b during May–June 1918, producing mixed results. *Lt.* Umlauff, the *Idflieg* cannon expert who visited various units to demonstrate the new weapon, flew Albatros J.I 734/17 on six missions over the front, but was severely wounded by an enemy fighter while attached to *Schlachtstaffel* 17. The "expedient" fuselage mounting was criticized because the side location restricted the field of fire, which depended too much on aircraft position and attitude in relation to the target. In addition, it was impossible to repair stoppages aloft. *Schlachtstaffel* 28b, experiencing problems with stoppages and handling the 15-round magazine, was convinced that a valuable weapon would result from adoption of belt-fed ammunition. *Schlachtstaffeln* 10 reported no gun stoppages, but noted the ammunition clip did not function smoothly and the side mounting restricted the field of fire. Moreover, accurate aiming was difficult because the tracer and explosive ammunition exhibited different ballistic characteristics. The *Schlachtstaffeln* expressed the unanimous opinion that the effectiveness of cannon-armed ground-attack aircraft depended wholly on keeping enemy fighters at bay.

Kofl 6 reported that in 12 missions the cannon had proved extremely effective, especially in dawn or dusk attacks on rear-area transportation, and more cannon-armed aircraft were urgently requested. For destroying tanks it was suggested that armor-piercing ammunition be supplied. The recommendation to install the cannon on a pivot

Frontbestand Class J Armored Infantry Aircraft Frontline Inventory

Manufacturer and Type		1914			1915					1916					1917					1918			
		31 Aug	31 Oct	31 Dec	28 Feb	30 Apr	30 Jun	31 Aug	31 Oct	31 Dec	28 Feb	30 Apr	30 Jun	31 Aug	31 Oct	31 Dec	28 Feb	30 Apr	30 Jun	31 Aug	31 Oct	31 Dec	28 Feb	30 Apr	30 Jun	31 Aug
AEG	J.I																		4	1	11	35	55	66	43	28
	J.II																								15	65	63
	J.																			3							
Albatros	J.I																						37	42	33	51	16
	J.II																										19
Junkers	J.I																				1	1	4	16	25	25	60
Total:																			7	2	12	76	113	139	184	186

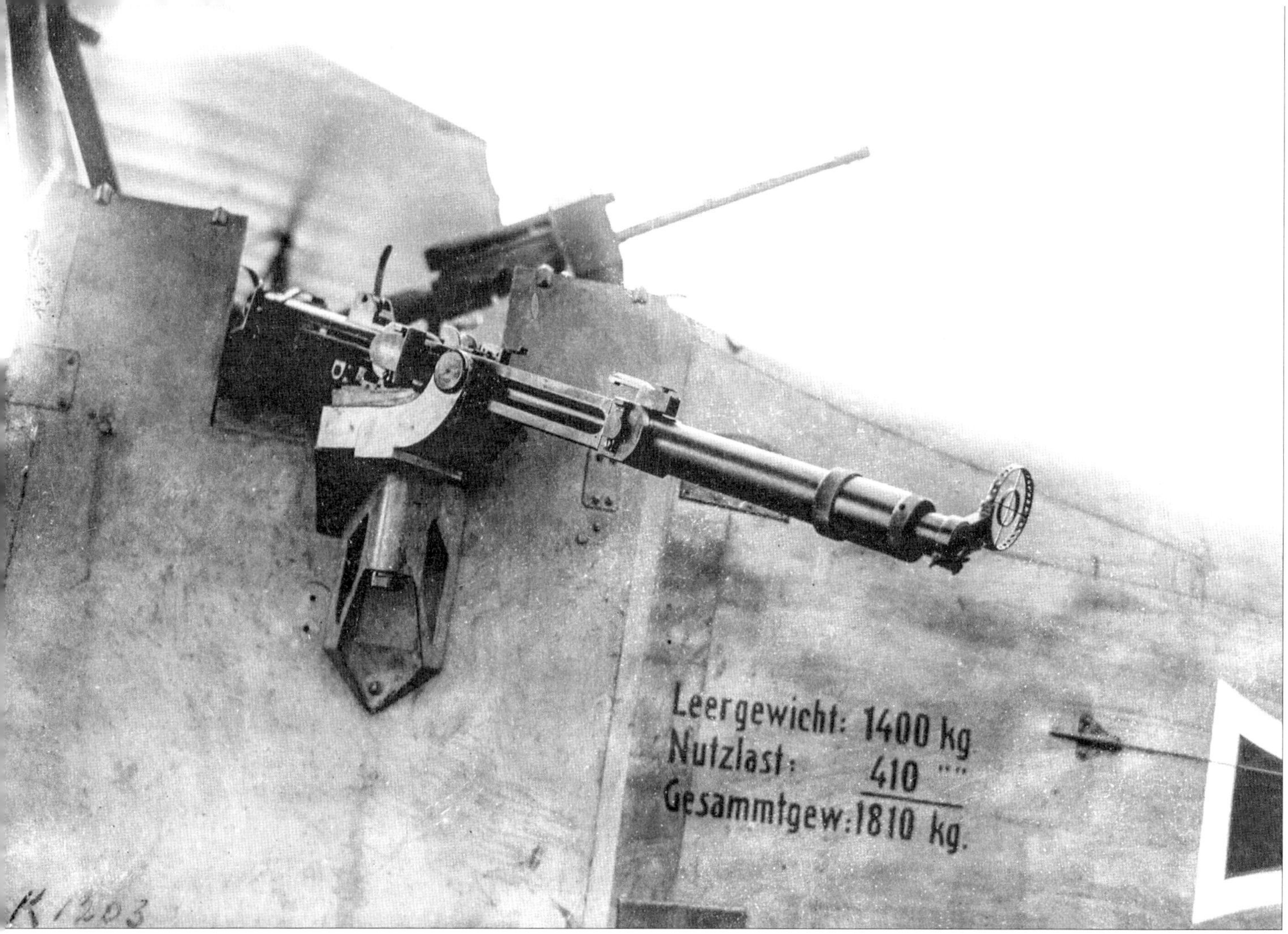

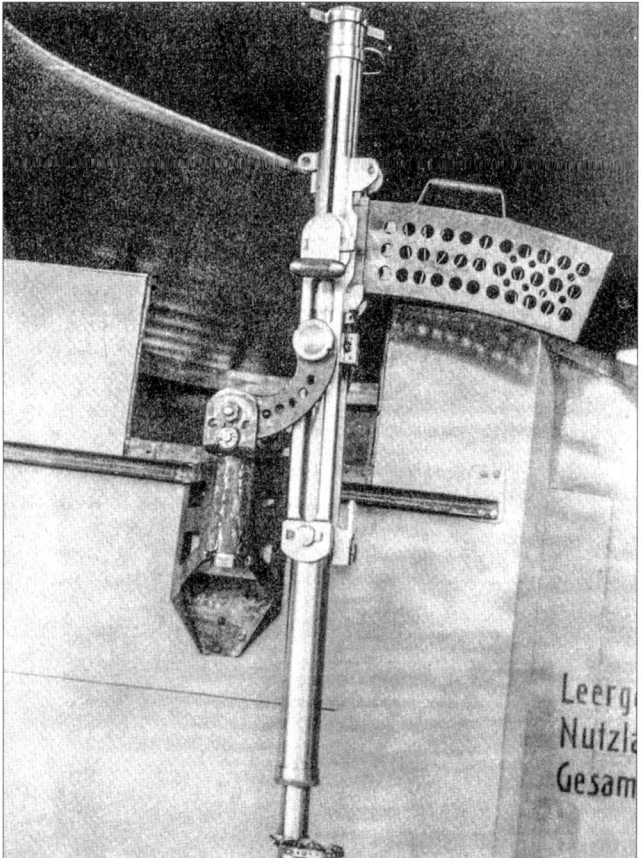

Above & Left: Some Albatros J.I aircraft mounted a 20mm Becker cannon on the left side of the aircraft for ground attack, and especially destroying tanks, as shown here. These experiments were successful enough to lead to development of improved cannon mounts for the Albatros J.II and AEG J.II, and eventually to more sophisticated anti-tank designs like the AEG G.IVk and Ago S.I. Decades later anti-tank helicopters were designed to fulfill the role pioneered by these little-known aircraft.

mount in the cockpit floor was accepted and tested in at least one Albatros J.I. On 11 June 1918, the first Albatros J.I with a Becker cannon, J.768/17, was forced down in enemy lines by ground fire.

In December 1917, three Albatros J.I without engines were purchased by the *k.u.k. Luftfahrtruppe*, as Series 09, and received the serial numbers 09.01–09.03. Originally, Albatros J.I 09.01 carried the German *Militär-Nummer* J.400/17; 90.02 was formerly J.726/17, and 90.03 was formerly J.730/17. Marta-built 250 hp Benz engines were installed. On 28 February 1918, aircraft 09.02 crashed in flames during evaluation tests at Aspern. On 5 May 1918, aircraft 09.01 was damaged at the front and returned to Aspern for repairs. The only J.I used operationally by the *Luftfahrtruppe* was 09.03, which served with *Flik* 69/S between July and September 1918.

Above: Albatros J.I J.738/17 of the second production batch has two-color camouflage over all upper surfaces and a white 'V' identification marking. (Courtesy Reinhard Zankl)

Above: This view of an early-production Albatros J.I shows the upper surface camouflage pattern. (Peter M. Grosz Collection/SDTB)

Above: Albatros J.I J.424/17 was the last aircraft of the first production batch. Here it has been repainted in 1918 insignia. Some of the engine cowling panels have been removed, possibly for maintenance, and it still retains its spinner. (Peter M. Grosz Collection/SDTB)

Below: An early production Albatros J.I with spinner, probably J.411/17, in 1918 insignia. (Peter M. Grosz Collection/SDTB)

Above: Albatros J.I J.714/17 of the second production batch in original 1917 insignia. (Peter M. Grosz Collection/SDTB)

Below: Albatros J.I J.745/17 of the second production batch has lasted long enough in service to be repainted with 1918 insignia. A dark band is painted around the fuselage and a recognition streamer is attached to the wing. The white background for the tail insignia extends onto the fin. (Peter M. Grosz Collection/SDTB)

Above & Below: Albatros J.I J.714/17 of the second production batch after a bad landing. J.714/17 is in factory finish with no special markings. The light gray armor around the cockpit is notable and the door providing easier access for the pilot is hanging open. The tubular container under the starboard lower wing is interesting. (AL0613-010 & AL0613-012)

Albatros J.I

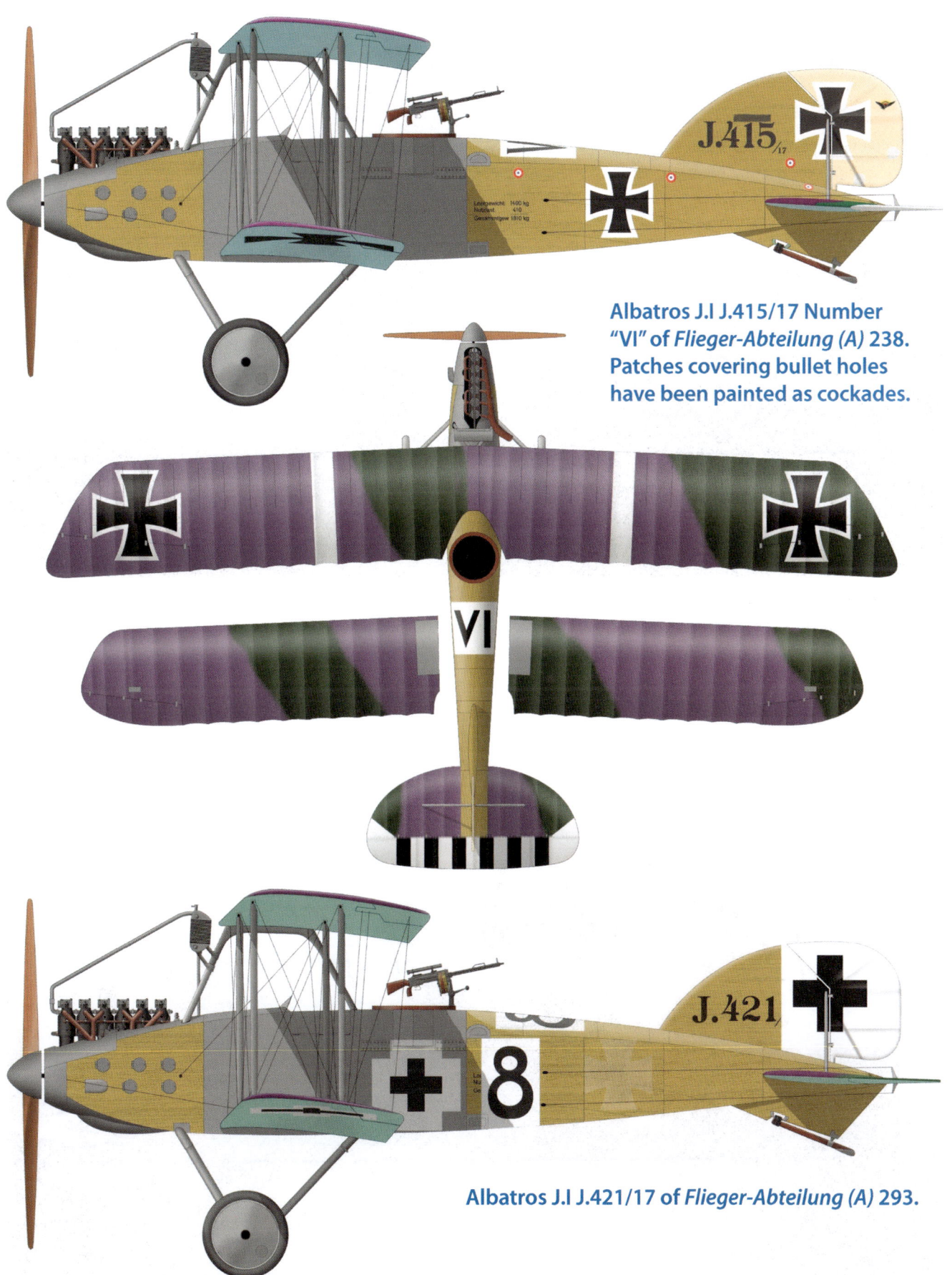

Albatros J.I J.415/17 Number "VI" of *Flieger-Abteilung (A) 238*. Patches covering bullet holes have been painted as cockades.

Albatros J.I J.421/17 of *Flieger-Abteilung (A) 293*.

Above: This Albatros J.I may be from the second production batch; it has no spinner but does not appear to have printed camouflage fabric. It has been painted overall dark camouflage colors, probably green and lilac like other Albatros two-seaters, with white nose, nose stripe, and letter 'L', probably at *Flieger-Abteilung (A)* 233 where it was serving when photographed.

Below: Closeup of an Albatros J.I radiator reveals that it was not armored. Together with its totally exposed location, that made it especially vulnerable to ground-fire. Engine failure could be expected two–three minutes after radiator puncture. Use of a box radiator instead of an airfoil radiator like that of the C.XII did nothing to improve performance of the J.I.

Above: Early production Albatros J.I with spinner, perhaps at Adlershof. Wind tunnel investigations eventually revealed that eliminating the spinner and rounding the nose actually reduced drag, and subsequent production J.I aircraft had no spinner. The same change was made to more well-known aircraft like the Rumpler C.IV and late-production Albatros D.III fighters built in Austria-Hungary.

Right: Closeup of an Albatros J.I showing details of the armor, the wood rear fuselage, and the gunner with his flexible machine gun. The J.I had little of the grace of the elegant Albatros C.XII from which it was derived.

Above: This Albatros J.I serving with *Flieger Abteilung* 33 is likely from the second production batch.
Below: The fuselage of Albatros J.I J.707/17 is moved the old-fashioned army way, soldier power.

Albatros J.I

Albatros J.I J.706/17.

Albatros J.I J.738/17.

Albatros J.I "L" of *Flieger-Abteilung (A) 233*.

Above: Albatros J.I J.706/17 is from the second production batch. In addition to the factory finish it carries a dark, probably black, zig-zag marking on the rear fuselage and tactical number '9'.

Above: This Albatros J.I with no spinner is likely from the second production batch.

Below: This Albatros J.I is likely from the second production batch and may be the same aircraft in the photo above.

Above: This Albatros J.I, tactical letter 'H', has experienced a bad landing. Downward-firing guns were installed.

Right: The cockpits of an Albatros J.I; the pilot's control wheel and side doors of armor are visible along with some details of the observer's cockpit.

Above: Albatros J.I J.727/17 of the second production batch wears only factory finish and markings.

Below: A derelict Albatros J.I appears to be the victim of artillery shelling or a bombing raid.

Above: Albatros J.I J.758/17 is shown with crew in this excellent portrait. Did 'Teddy' (rear inboard strut) fly any missions?

Above: Albatros J.I J.756/17 poses with ground crew. Two downward-firing guns are visible.

Left: Albatros J.I poses with its flight crew.

Albatros J.I

Above: Colorized photo of Albatros J.I J.758/17 with crew in this excellent portrait courtesy of Jim Miller.

Albatros J.I J.758/17.

Above: As war reparations several German aircraft were sent to Japan, where a contemporary artist painted details of their camouflage, which are reproduced above for the J.I.

Above, Above Right, & Below: These gruesome photos of the demise of Albatros J.I J.769/17 were found in an album from Spa 150, suggesting a Spad from that unit downed the J.I and its unfortunate crew. The photos are dated 11 June 1918.

Albatros J.I

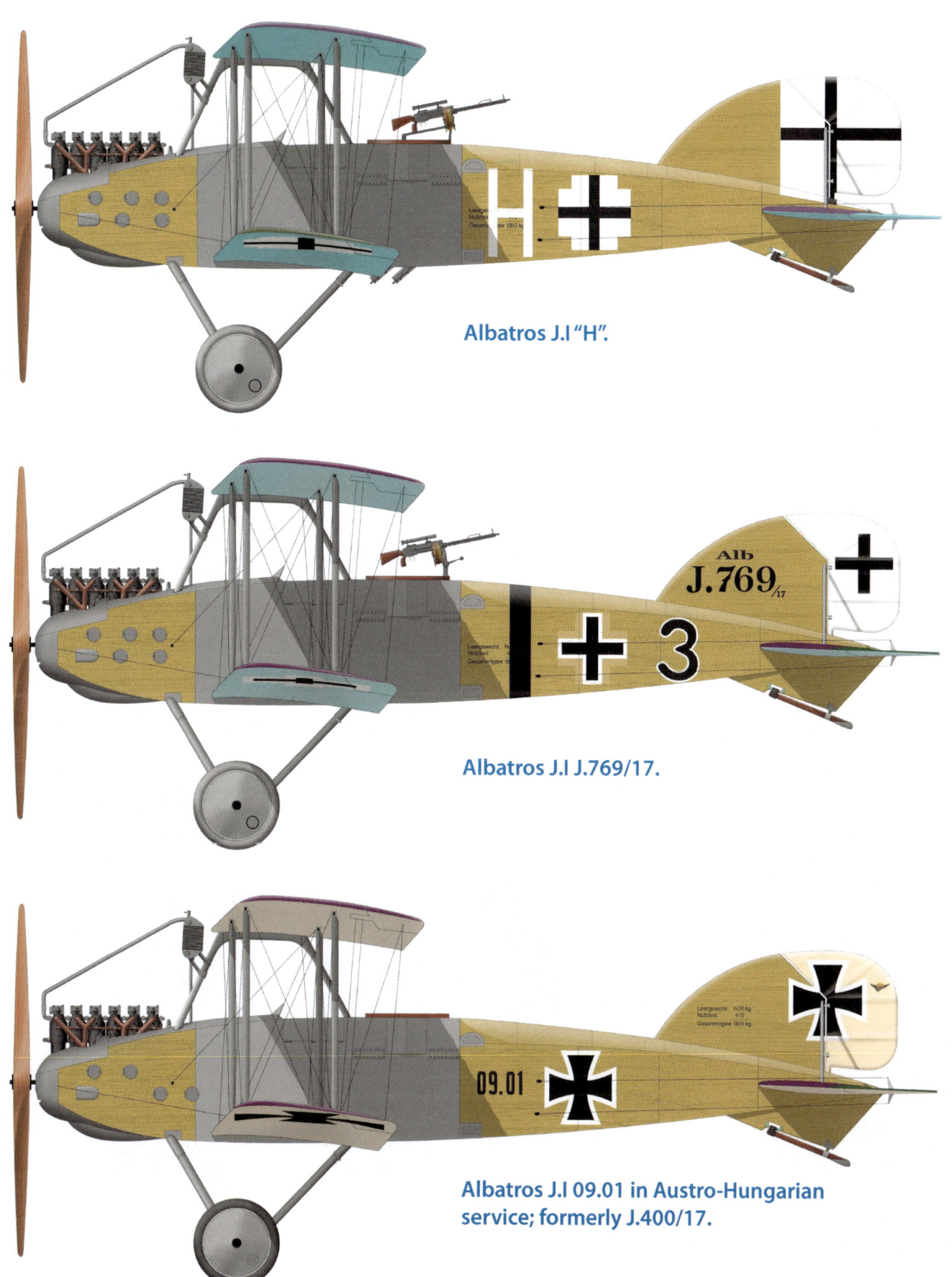

Albatros J.I "H".

Albatros J.I J.769/17.

Albatros J.I 09.01 in Austro-Hungarian service; formerly J.400/17.

Above & Below: Albatros J.I 09.03 was the last of three purchased by Austria-Hungary. Formerly J.730/17, 09.03 was the only J.I used operationally by the *Luftfahrtruppe;* it served with *Flik* 69/S between July and September 1918. The two-color camouflage painted on the upper surface of the wings and tailplane is evident below.

Above & Below: Albatros J.I 09.01 was formerly German *Militär-Nummer* J.400/17. Marta-built 250 hp Benz engines were installed. On 5 May 1918 Albatros J.I 09.01 was damaged at the front before seeing operations and returned to Aspern for repairs. It no longer has its 'as-built' propeller spinner. Below a Brandenburg C.I is in the background. (AL0613-002)

Above: Albatros J.I J.742/17 of the second production batch crashed in 1918. A white "X" was the identifying marking just forward of the fuselage national insignia.

Facing Page, Top & Bottom: Two views of an early-production Albatros J.I with propeller spinner; unfortunately, the aircraft is not identified but may be J.411/17.

Below: An Albatros J.I is the center of attention for this group of officers and officials.

29

Above: Albatros J.I J.711/17 provides a background for this photograph of members of *Flieger Abteilung (A) 257*.

Albatros J.I J.745/17 of an unknown unit, 1918.

Above: Post-war the new Polish state used a number of German warplanes, including the Albatros J.I. As can be seen on its fin, this J.I, named *Smok* and with tactical number '6', wears the irregular camouflage pattern illustrated by the Japanese artist in color on the top of page 24.

Albatros J.I "6" *Smok*, post-war Polish Air Service.

Above & Below: Polish Albatros J.I tactical number '6', apparently before it was named. The photo above shows the irregular camouflage pattern on its fuselage. The photo below is too dark to show the pattern clearly but does show the printed camouflage fabric on the wings and horizontal tail surfaces. The serial, J.I 217/18, does not correspond to known serial numbers for the Albatros J.I.

Albatros J.II

Above: The Albatros J.II was redesigned to improve survivability in the hostile environment in which it flew its missions. Most importantly, the entire engine was now armored, solving the worst problem with the J.I. In addition, unlike the J.I, the radiator was now armored, further improving survivability. Finally, the upper ailerons were given aerodynamic horn balances to reduce control pressures for better maneuverability. The same basic Benz engine was used, but power was boosted 10% to 220 hp to compensate for the greater weight of the engine armor, which accounted for the boxy cowling. The result was a more robust, survivable aircraft with essentially the same performance despite its greater weight.

Although the Albatros J.I met the letter of the J-type requirement for armor protection of the crew, it was the only production J-type that did not have an armored engine. Unsurprisingly, lack of engine armor was the flyers' main complaint about the Albatros J.I, leading directly to the redesigned J.II. Like the competing Junkers and AEG designs, the Albatros J.II featured armor around the engine, giving the J.II a boxy nose instead of the streamlined nose of the Albatros J.I. In addition, the radiator was likewise armored to make it less vulnerable.

To compensate for the additional weight of the engine armor, the J.II had the 220 hp Benz Bz.IVa, a slightly more powerful version of the 200 hp Benz Bz.IV engine installed in the J.I. Wing sweep was reduced slightly to maintain proper center of gravity with the additional nose armor. Despite the additional power, maximum speed of the J.II remained the same as the J.I due to the increase in weight and drag – a slow 140 km/h. Like the preceding Albatros J.I, climb and ceiling of the J.II remained modest. Nevertheless, since most missions were flown at 500 meters or less, climb rate and ceiling were not viewed as critical for J-type aircraft, which relied on their armor for protection instead of speed and altitude performance.

Like the preceding C.XII and J.I, the J.II had ailerons on all four wings. However, to reduce control forces and improve responsiveness, the upper wings of the J.II were given horn-balanced

Above: Albatros J.II at the factory, perhaps 127/18. Despite its boxy shape due to construction from armored plates, care has been taken to minimize frontal area to keep drag in check. Two fixed guns firing downward protrude from the bottom of the fuselage. A guard shack painted in stripes is in the right background and the airship hangar is behind the aircraft.

Below: Another view of the same Albatros J.II shows more of its nose. With its armored engine and radiator, the J.II was much more likely to survive being hit by rifle-caliber ground fire than its J.I predecessor.

ailerons. Tail surfaces remained the same as the J.I. Initially, armament was also the same; a flexible machine gun for the observer and two fixed machine guns firing downward at a 45° angle. However, the Albatros J.II was designed to carry a flexible 20mm Becker cannon mounted in the floor of the observer's cockpit. But *Idflieg* reported that, by the end of September 1918, no J.II aircraft carrying this armament had been delivered. Forward-firing armament had not been installed on J-type aircraft because it was not considered useful for air-to-air combat given the heavy J-type's lack of agility. Likewise, diving at ground targets for strafing was at first considered too risky for these heavy, armored aircraft. However, due to difficulty aiming the downward-firing guns, as J.II production progressed the two fixed guns reportedly were moved to the conventional position in front of the pilot and firing directly ahead. If so, it was the only J-type to use this armament configuration. Unfortunately, photographs to confirm this installation have not surfaced.

While the Albatros J.II had better armor protection than the J.I, its greater weight with essentially the same wing further increased its stall speed and aggravated the take-off distance, agility, and flight safety challenges suffered by all J-types. Albatros J.II production orders totaled 150 aircraft.

Above Right: The 20mm Becker cannons fitted to the Albatros J.Is proved to be effective anti-tank weapons, and 20 Albatros J.II aircraft were fitted with these weapons in an improved mount in the floor of the gunner's cockpit shown here; the front of the aircraft is at the top of the photo. Extra magazines for the Becker are stacked on the sides of the armored cockpit and extra drums of machine gun ammunition are stored at the rear. Twenty AEG J.II aircraft were delivered with a similar Becker installation.

Below: Albatros J.II 127/18 is shown here in its basic factory finish and markings. Flying surfaces are covered with printed camouflage fabric, the armor is painted light gray, and the wood rear fuselage and fin are clear-varnished.

Above: Some Albatros J.II aircraft had the fuselage camouflage seen on some J.I aircraft and illustrated in color by the Japanese artist on page 24. No unit or personal markings are visible; the tires are missing due to the rubber shortage.

Below: This postwar view of German aircraft sent to Italy as reparations shows an Albatros J.II in the middle with the same pattern of fuselage camouflage seen above, another indication it was applied at the factory.

Above: Albatros J.II 126/18 serves in basic factory finish and markings; no unit or personal markings are visible.

Above: This rear view of the Albatros J.II displays its standard factory finish and markings. Printed camouflage fabric covers all flying surfaces, the armor is painted light gray, and the wood rear fuselage and fin are varnished.

Above: Albatros J.II ready for a mission clearly showing the downward-firing guns and observer's flexible gun. The wind-driven dynamo for the wireless is on the front undercarriage strut, and the leads for the antenna are below the fuselage.

Facing Page: Albatros J.II after a landing accident; the downward-firing guns are barely visible under the fuselage.

Above: Albatros J.II ready for a mission.

Above: Albatros J.II 140/18 serves in basic factory finish and markings; no unit or personal markings are visible.

Albatros J.II, serial unknown.

Albatros J.II Factory Drawing

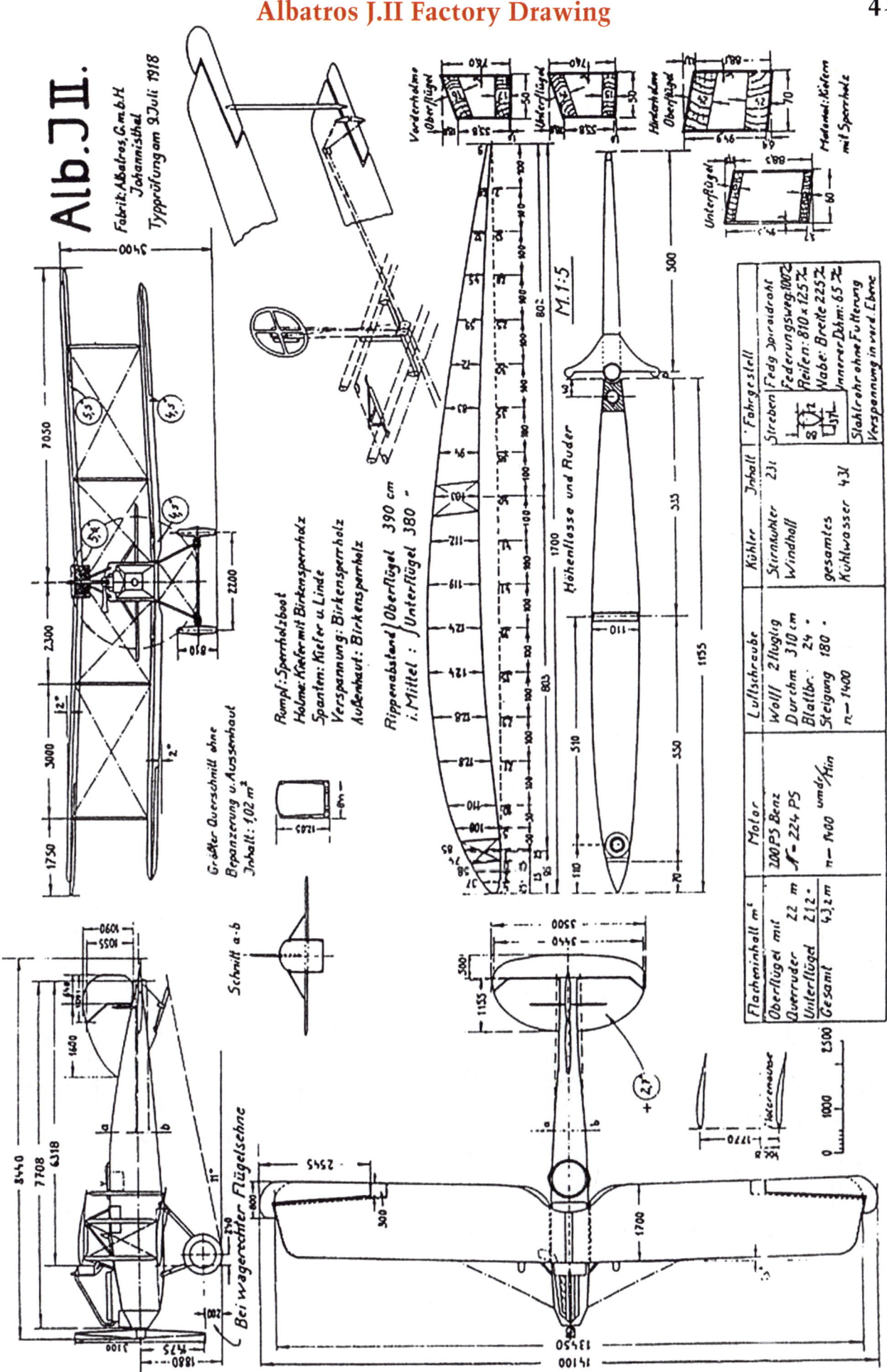

Albatros J.I & J.II

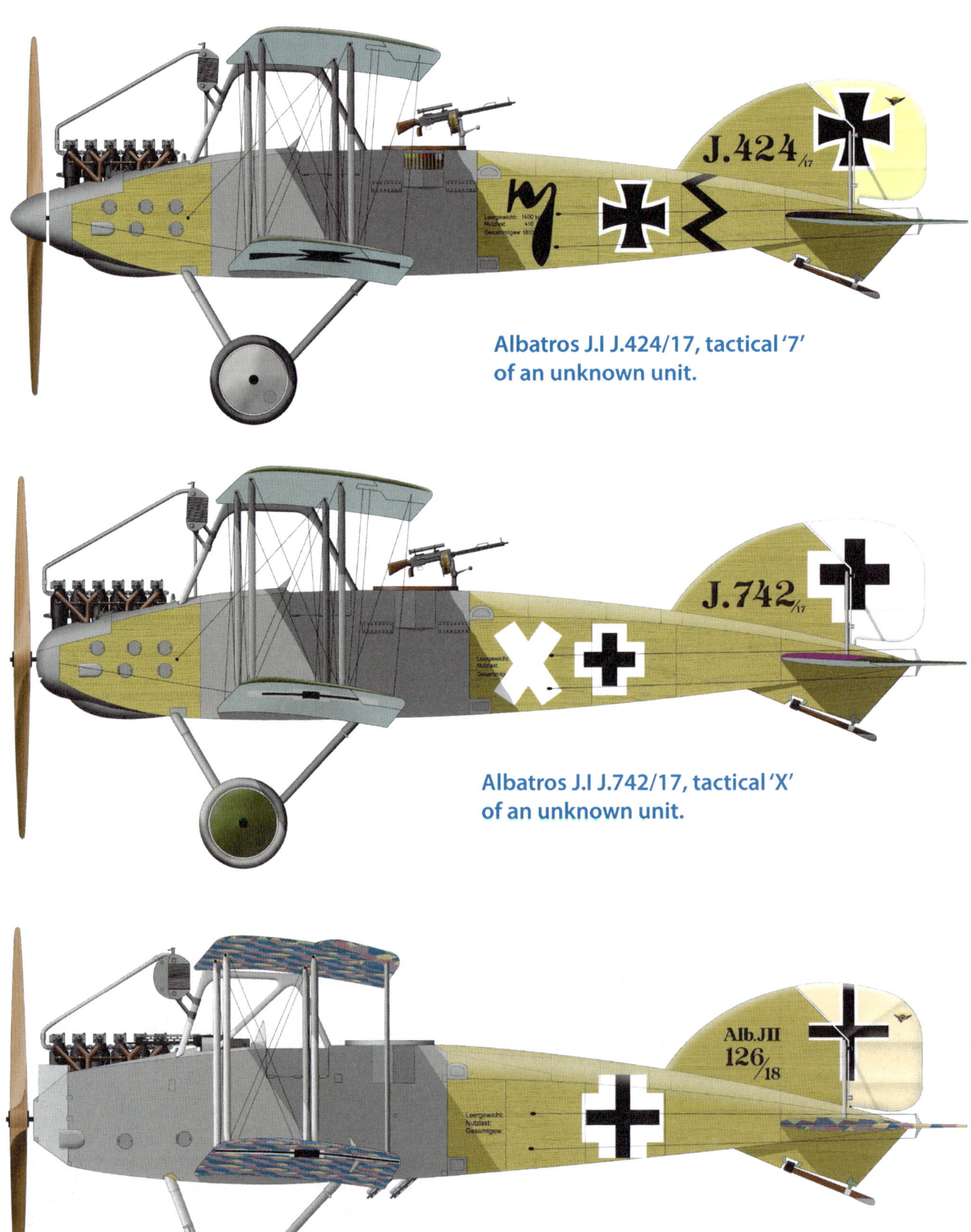

Albatros J.I J.424/17, tactical '7' of an unknown unit.

Albatros J.I J.742/17, tactical 'X' of an unknown unit.

Albatros J.II J.126/18. This aircraft was photographed either with no exhaust or the exhaust was angled downward.

Albatros J.II

Albatros J.II 127/18.

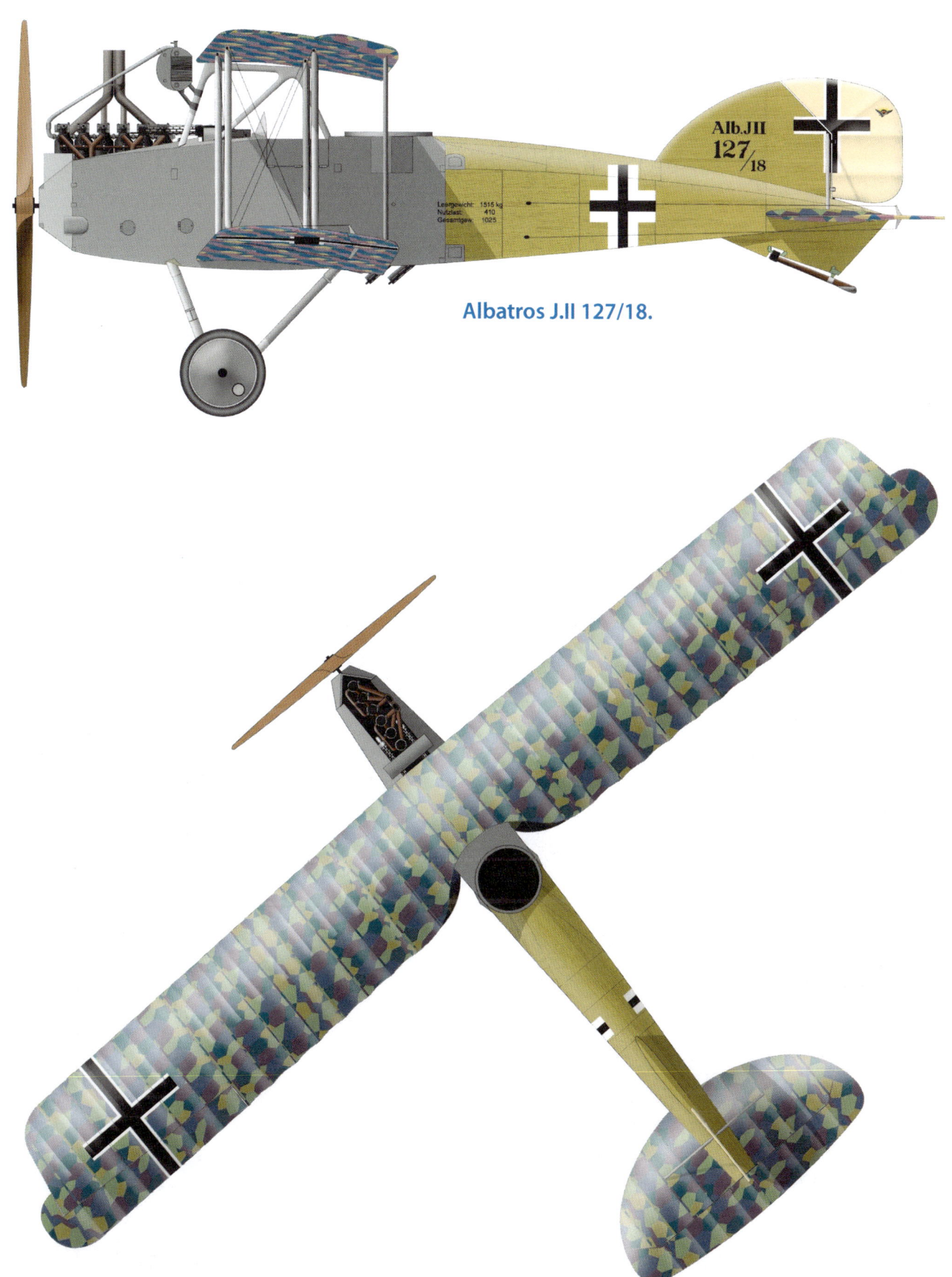

Albatros Bombers

The Albatros company was famous for its fighters and two-seat reconnaissance airplanes, but also designed several G-type bombers, of which one, the G.III, saw service. Of all the operational G-types, those designed by Albatros were built in the smallest numbers and served for the shortest period.

Albatros G.I

Above & Below: A single Albatros G.I was built but the type was not satisfactory. (Above: Peter M. Grosz Collection, SDTB)

Ostdeutsche Albatroswerke G.m.b.H (OAW), part of the Albatroswerke G.m.b.H, was one of two Albatros companies until they merged in October 1917. Chief engineer at OAW was *Dipl.-Ing.* Karl Grohmann, who designed the Albatros G.I. Only a single Albatros G.I was built at OAW's Schneidemühl factory. Interestingly, it was a rare, four-engine aircraft with three bays of bracing outboard of the tractor engines. The G.I was powered by four 120 hp Mercedes D.II engines and made its first flight on January 31, 1916, but no further details are available. For unknown reasons the aircraft was unsatisfactory and no further development was undertaken.

Albatros Bomber Specifications			
	G.I	**G.II**	**G.III**
Engines	4 x 120 hp Mercedes D.II	2 x 150 hp Benz Bz.III	2 x 220 hp Benz Bz.IV
Span (Upper)	30 m	17.0 m	18.0 m
Span (Lower)	—	17.0 m	17.0 m
Length	—	11.9 m	11.9 m
Height	—	4.2 m	4.2 m
Empty Weight	—	—	2,004 kg
Loaded Weight	4,319 kg	—	3,086 kg
Max. Speed	—	—	150 km/h
Climb, 1,000 m	—	9.3 minutes	10.0 minutes
Climb, 2,000 m	—	25 minutes	30 minutes
Climb, 3,000 m	—	70 minutes	45 minutes
Service Ceiling	—	3,000 m	3,000 m
Range/Endurance	—	4 hours	595 km
Bomb Load	—	—	325 kg
Armament	—	2 flexible MGs	2 flexible MGs

Note: Only one G.I and one G.II were built. The highest number of Albatros bombers at the front was 9, indicating a short production run. Known serials were in the range G.126–132/16.

Frontbeststand Inventory of G-Type Aircraft (Twin-Engine Bombers) at the Front

Manufacturer and Type		1914			1915					1916						1917					1918			
		31 Aug	31 Oct	31 Dec	28 Feb	30 Apr	30 Jun	31 Aug	31 Oct	31 Dec	28 Feb	30 Apr	30 Jun	31 Aug	31 Oct	31 Dec	28 Feb	30 Apr	30 Jun	31 Aug	31 Oct	31 Dec	28 Feb	30 Apr	30 Jun	31 Aug
AEG	G.I						1	5			5															
	G.II						2	5	10	13	12	2	4	4	4	2	2	1								
	G.III												6	16	22	21	22	9								
	G.IV									1								5	9	15	15	35	37	54	74	51
	G.																	3								
Albatros	G.II																1	9	1	1		1				
	G.III																	2	1	2						
Friedrichshafen	G.II														1		4	8	17	17	10	9	2	1	1	1
	G.III																	9	32	24	57	69	96	74	24	
	G.IIIa																							18	95	
	G.IV																							4	8	
	G.IVa																							5	6	
Gotha	G.I							5	6	1		1	1	1												
	G.II													4	3	1	1									
	G.III													7	14		3	4	3	3						
	G.IV															1		30	36	34	35	19	10	8	6	5
	G.V																		3	20	33	34	36	15	8	
	G.Va																						11	19	4	
	G.Vb																									21
Rumpler	G.I										1		1													
	G.II										1	7	8	4	1	1										
	G.III													1	3	5	5	10	1	4						
Total:							2	6	20	20	13	7	13	28	48	46	34	71	86	111	116	155	156	206	216	223

Above: Contrary to the *Frontbestand* above, the Albatros G.II remained a single prototype, and the inventory of G.II aircraft shown above were actually Albatros G.III aircraft; the numbers in the two rows should be combined under G.III.

Albatros G.II

Above: The sole Albatros G.II prototype was a compact bomber with thick airfoil, equal span wings. The engines were mounted as pushers above the lower wing in streamlined nacelles. A nose landing gear was fitted to prevent nose-overs.

At the main Albatros factory at Johannisthal, Robert Thelen, assisted by George Madelung, designed the two-engine Albatros G.II based on the *Kampfflugzeug* specificatins promulgated by *Idflieg* in July 1914. Madelung was responsible for the thick airfoil section chosen for the G.II that was intended to give it greater lift than the thin sections then common. The prototype C.IV was built specifically to test this thick airfoil section for the G.II.

The G.II fuselage was covered with plywood like other Albatros designs of that time and carried three crewmen, a pilot in the middle and fore and aft gunners. The massive interplane struts eliminated the need for incidence bracing wires and the landing gear resembled that of a two-seater except for the nose gear. With 150 hp Benz Bz.III engines the aircraft was reliable but under-powered, and interest moved on to a more powerful derivative, the G.III.

Left: The Albatros G.II was a compact, streamlined bomber with good flying characteristics. However, climb and ceiling were poor and it was evident that more power was needed than the 150 hp Benz Bz.III engines delivered. Design of the G.II was unrelated to the G.I other than company name.

Above: The sole Albatros G.II prototype under test at Johannisthal. Its thick airfoil, equal span wings, and massive single-bay interplane struts were hallmarks of this distinctive design.

Above: The sole Albatros G.II looked like a member of the Albatros family of aircraft with the exceptions of the thick airfoil and the balanced rudder needed to give more directional control in case of engine failure.

This Page & Facing Page: More images of the sole Albatros G.II prototype under test at Johannisthal. (Peter M. Grosz Collection/SDTB)

Albatros G.III

Above: This appears to be the Albatros G.III prototype. The engines are mounted above the lower wing in streamlined nacelles, the single-bay interplane struts are normal size, and the upper wing span has been increased but the ailerons have no aerodynamic balances. The G.III discarded the nose landing gear used by the G.II.

The Albatros G.III was based on the G.II and used a similar, perhaps identical, plywood-covered fuselage. More powerful engines, 220 hp Benz Bz.IV inline six-cylinder types, were fitted to improve climb and bombload. The thick airfoil section was retained, and to further improve load-carrying capability the upper wing span was increased by a meter for more lifting area. At first the ailerons were similar to those of the G.II, but later aerodynamic balances were fitted to reduced the pilot's control forces and improve maneuverability. However, the aerodynamic balance on the rudder was deleted, apparently to harmonize the control forces.

The landing gear was modified to eliminate the nose gear and dual wheels were fitted to each main gear. More conventional interplane bracing was used, although the G.III retained the single-bay configuration. Installation of the more powerful engines was similar to the G.II but the mounting was more streamlined. However, cooling problems must have afflicted the G.III because nearly all photos of operational G.III bombers show them without any cowling panels for improved cooling at the expense of streamlining.

Despite the improvements compared to the G.II, the G.III still had a lighter bomb load than its rivals and its flying and landing characteristics were not as good as desired. Regardless, *Idflieg* ordered a small number of G.III bombers, perhaps 10–12, for operational evaluation. In early 1917 some were assigned to *Kagohl* 4 in the Balkans, and others were assigned to *Kagohl* 2 on the Western Front. The G.III front-line inventory peaked at nine aircraft in April and only one was at the front by the end of 1917.

The Albatros G.III thus made a limited contribution to the German war effort and was the least successful operational bomber. Its qualities were such that Albatros abandoned further development of two-engine bombers to focus on their more successful fighters and two-seaters.

Above: This appears to be the prototype Albatros G.III after the ailerons were fitted with aerodynamic balances to reduce the control forces. The G.III was streamlined for a 1916 two-engine bomber. The thick airfoil section for high lift, unusual for an Albatros design, is clearly evident.

Above: This rear quarter view of the Albatros G.III prototype emphasizes its aerodynamic design for a two-engine bomber of the period. The engines are mounted in streamlined nacelles, the wing bracing is single-bay, and the landing gear is simple. The tail surfaces are shaped like the successful, contemporary Albatros two-seaters and fighters, although the fuselage was rectangular in cross section, unlike Albatros fighters with their oval fuselage designs. The G.III had three crewmen, a pilot and fore and aft gunners, and each gunner had a single, flexible machine gun. The thick airfoil section was chosen for high lift and within Albatros designs was unique to the G.II, G.III, and the C.IV airfoil testbed. Flight testing led to addition of aerodynamic balances on the ailerons to reduce control forces and improve maneuverability. The number of Albatros G.III bombers built is not known; but the maximum front-line inventory was nine in April 1917.

Above & Below: Albatros G.III, likely the prototype, undergoing winter testing with its engine cowlings fitted. Bomb racks are visible under the center section. (Peter M. Grosz Collection/SDTB)

Above & Below: Albatros G.III, likely the prototype, undergoing winter testing with its engine cowlings fitted. The bomb racks are clearly visible on the fuselage sides in both photos and under the center section in the photo above. (Peter M. Grosz Collection/SDTB)

Above & Below: Two views of a winter landing accident. The aircraft, likely the prototype, had its engine cowlings fitted. The starboard landing gear was torn from the aircraft during the accident. This appears to be the same aircraft and accident shown in the winter accident scene on page 157. (Peter M. Grosz Collection/SDTB)

Albatros G.III

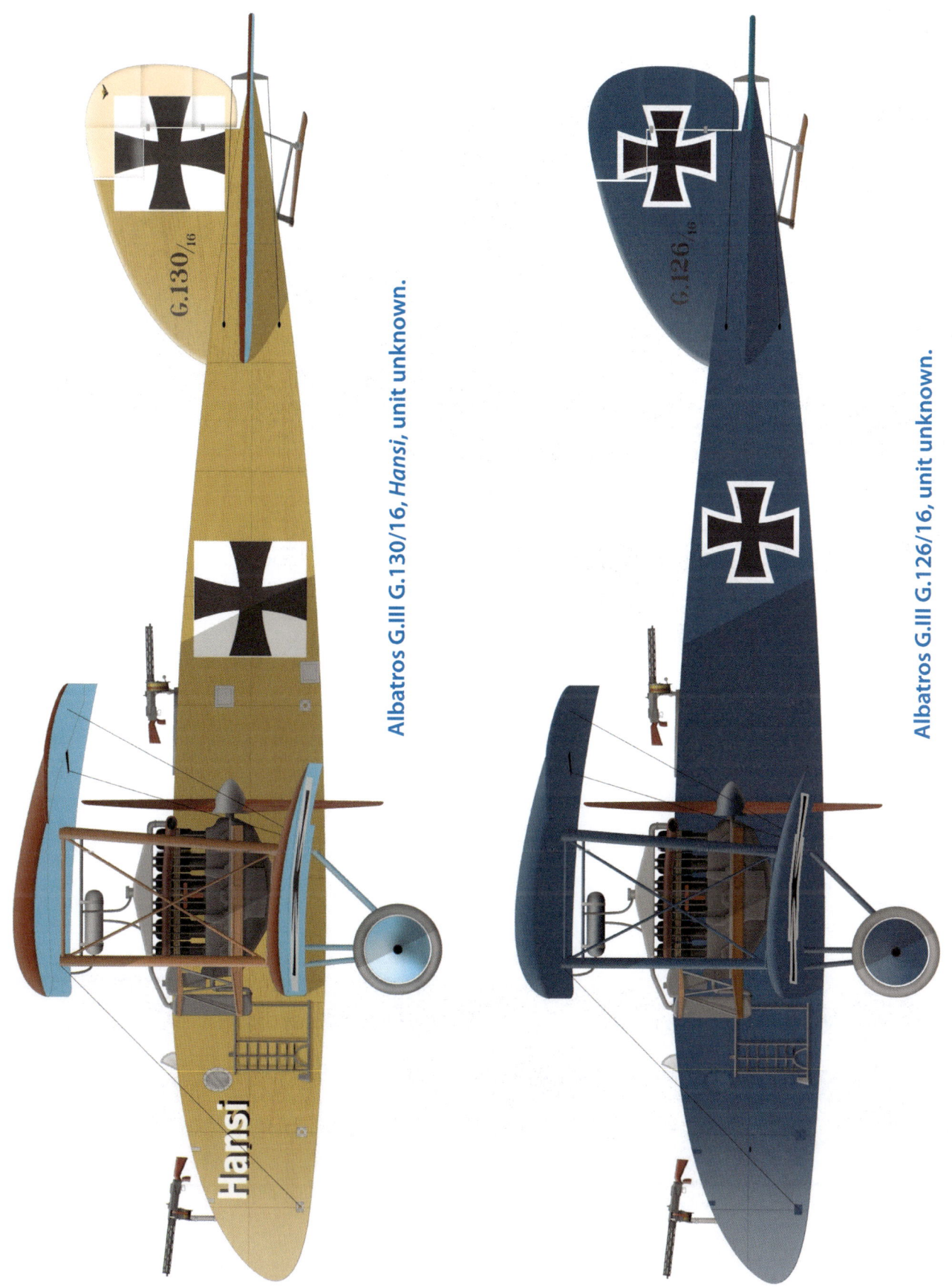

Albatros G.III G.130/16, *Hansi*, unit unknown.

Albatros G.III G.126/16, unit unknown.

Facing Page & Right: Albatros G.III in dark colors displays its bomb load. Six heavier bombs (in this case apparently 50 kg *P.u.W.* bombs) are carried under the fuselage near the center of gravity and smaller (12.5 kg *P.u.W.*) bombs are carried in racks on the fuselage sides. The bomb load could total at least 325 kg, and this G.III appears to be carrying more than that.

Above & Below: Landing accidents with two different Albatros G.III bombers had similar results. The aircraft above was flying in summer and the engine cowlings had been removed, while the aircraft below, likely the prototype, was flying in winter and had its engine cowlings fitted.

Left & Below: Albatros G.III G.130/16 *Hansi* at an operational unit. The thick airfoil section and aerodynamically-balanced ailerons are unlike other contemporary Albatros warplanes, but the shape of the tail surfaces is very similar to that of contemporary Albatros fighters and two-seaters.

Below: Albatros G.III G.132/16 at an operational unit is the center of a lot of attention as well as a popular background for group photographs.

Above & Below: Albatros G.III G.132/16 at an operational unit. The thick airfoil section – unlike other contemporary Albatros warplanes – and fuselage bomb racks are prominent. The spinners are missing and the engine cowlings have been removed for improved cooling despite the increased drag produced. Above some nurses are being given a guided tour of the aircraft.

Above & Below: Albatros G.III G.126/16 serving with an operational unit. The thick airfoil section is prominent as are the bomb racks. Although the spinners have been retained, the engine cowling has been removed for additional cooling. The wood grain of the ply-covered fuselage is noticeable in the photo above, but appears to have been painted in the photo below, probably for duty as a night bomber because the paint appears as dark as the national insignia under the wing, but lighter on the fuselage, probably as a result of the sunlight.

Above: Another photo of Albatros G.III G.132/16 at an operational unit. The spinners are missing and the engine cowlings have been removed for improved cooling despite the increased drag produced.

Below: Due to its dark finish this Albatros G.III appears to be from an operational unit and crashed on the railroad tracks, perhaps while attempting an emergency landing. (Peter M. Grosz Collection/SDTB)

Left: Aircrew and others relax around their Albatros G.III bomber with its engine cowlings removed. The fact nearly all photos show the G.III without engine cowlings indicates cooling problems.

Below: Aircrew and visitors relax around an Albatros G.III bomber in the field. Like most photos showing operational G.III bombers, it has had its engine cowlings removed.

Below: This G.III, likely the prototype, had its engine cowlings removed even when flying in winter.

Albatros WDD

63

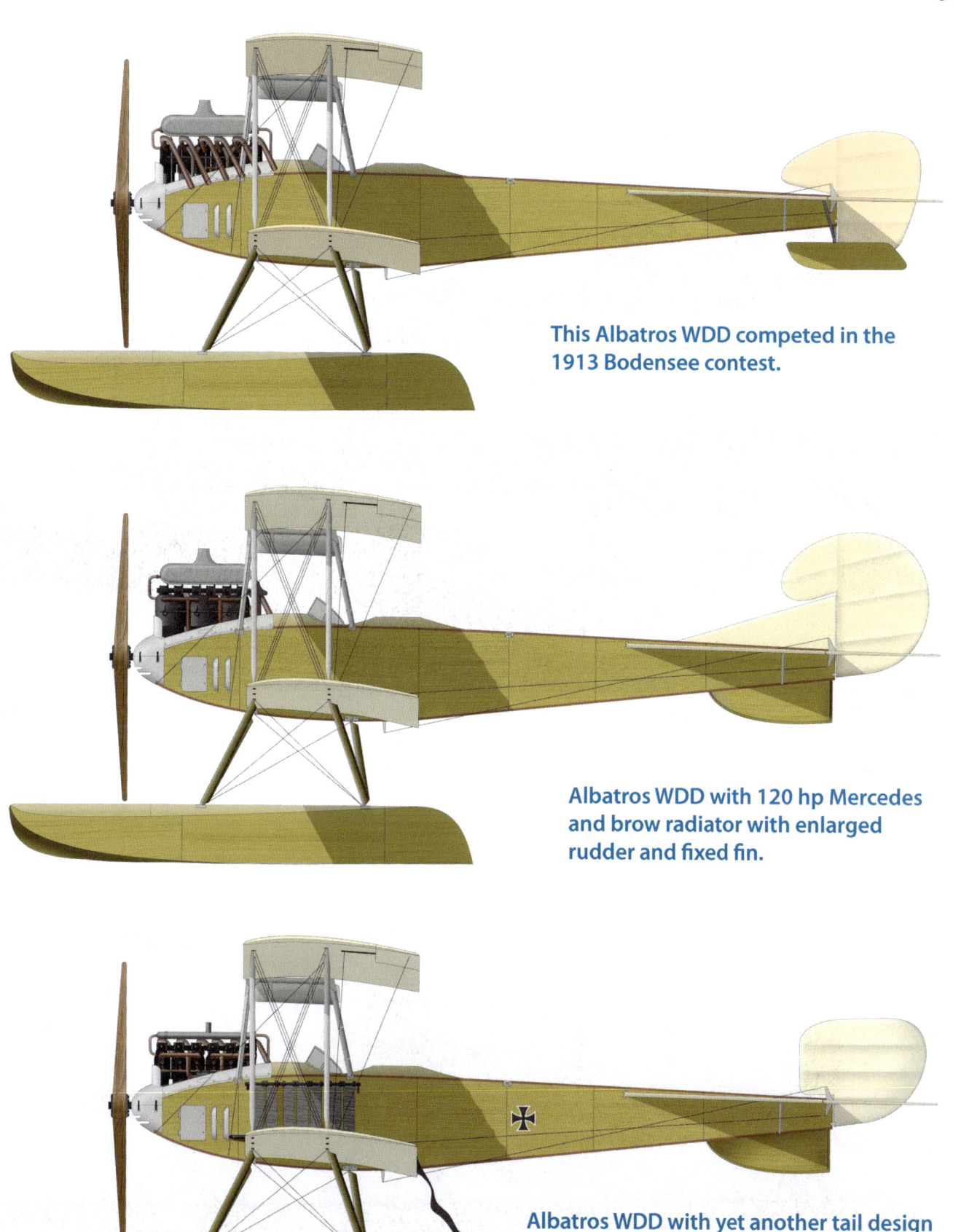

This Albatros WDD competed in the 1913 Bodensee contest.

Albatros WDD with 120 hp Mercedes and brow radiator with enlarged rudder and fixed fin.

Albatros WDD with yet another tail design and small national insignia on the fuselage. Side radiators have replaced the brow radiator used on earlier WDDs.

Albatros Seaplanes

Albatros built a small number of miscellaneous seaplanes before the war and early in the war, some designed by other manufacturers. Albatros also designed the W.3 and follow-on W.5 torpedo bombers and three prototypes of the W.8 two-seat floatplane fighter. However, the majority of Albatros floatplane production was of the W.4 single-seat floatplane fighter, a floatplane development of the successful Albatros D.I Army fighter. Initially the Navy purchased single-seat floatplane fighters for defense of naval air stations and limited offensive operations, and the Albatros W.4 was produced in greater numbers than the competing Brandenburg KDW and Rumpler 6B1 in the same class.

From its experience with single-seat floatplane fighters the Navy decided to adopt two-seat floatplane fighters for greater combat effectiveness, especially in longer-range offensive operations. Here the Brandenburg W.12 succeeded brilliantly and set the pace and configuration for all subsequent floatplane fighters, including the Albatros W.8, of which only three prototypes were built.

The *SVK* table reproduced below shows Albatros seaplane orders and deliveries; it clearly shows that W.4 production dominated Albatros seaplane production during the war.

SVK Table of Albatros Seaplane Orders and Deliveries

Order Number	Type	Marine Numbers	Design	Class & Engine	1914 J F M A M J J A S O N D	1915 J F M A M J J A S O N D
1		2/3		70	Delivered in February 1912, struck off charge By Order 8954/13	
2		5	O.S	95Nag	Delivered in February 1912, struck off charge By Order 976/14	
3		9/11		100Arg	Delivered in February 1912, struck off charge By Order 8954/13	
4		14		100M	Delivered in February 1912, struck off charge By Order 8954/13	
5		16		95Nag	Delivered in February 1912, struck off charge By Order 6216/14	
6		17		100M	Delivered in February 1912, struck off charge By Order 6216/13	
7		20/24		100M	Order and Delivery Not Determined	
8		40			Order and Delivery Not Determined	
9		52/56		150B	Order by Take-over 2 2 1	
10		74	B	150B	1	
11		111		100M	1	
12		221/230	K.351 B	150B	10	3 1 4 1
13		432	B	100M	2	1
14		433/435			These Numbers Are Cancelled	
15		446/447	K.361 B	160M		Order Not Determined 1
16		450	W.2 C	160M		1
17	527	527	W.3 T	2x150B		1
18	747	747	W.4 ED	160M		
19	747	785/786	W.4 ED	160M		
20	847	845/849	W.5 T	2x150B		
21	911	902/911	W.4 ED	160M		
22	949	948/967	W.4 ED	160M		
23	949	1107/1116	W.4 ED	160M		
24	949	1302/1326	W.4 ED	160M		
25	949	1484/1503	W.4 ED	160M		
26	949	1504/1513	W.4 ED	160M		
27	949	1719/1738	W.4 ED	160M		
28	5002	5001/5003	W.8	C3MG 195B		
Orders that Month					1 10 2 2	1 1
Deliveries that Month					2 2 1 1 1	3 1 4 1 2 1
Orders that Year					15	2
Orders: 3 Deliveries: 2 Deliveries that Year					7	12

Albatros W.1–W.8 Seaplane Production

Aircraft	Number Built	Marine Numbers
Albatros W.1	19	52–56, 74, 111, 221–230, 432, 446
Albatros W.2	1	450
Albatros W.3	1	527
Albatros W.4	118	747, 785–786, 902–911, 948–967, 1107–1116, 1302–1326, 1484–1503, 1504–1513, 1719–1738
Albatros W.5	5	845–849
Albatros W.8	3	5001–5003

Note: The early Albatros seaplanes are not clearly documented in the SVK tables. The Marine Numbers listed for the W.1 include those originally designated WDD (52–56 & 74) and those potentially W.1 (111, 221–230, 432, 446) with no type specified or specified as K.351 and K.361.

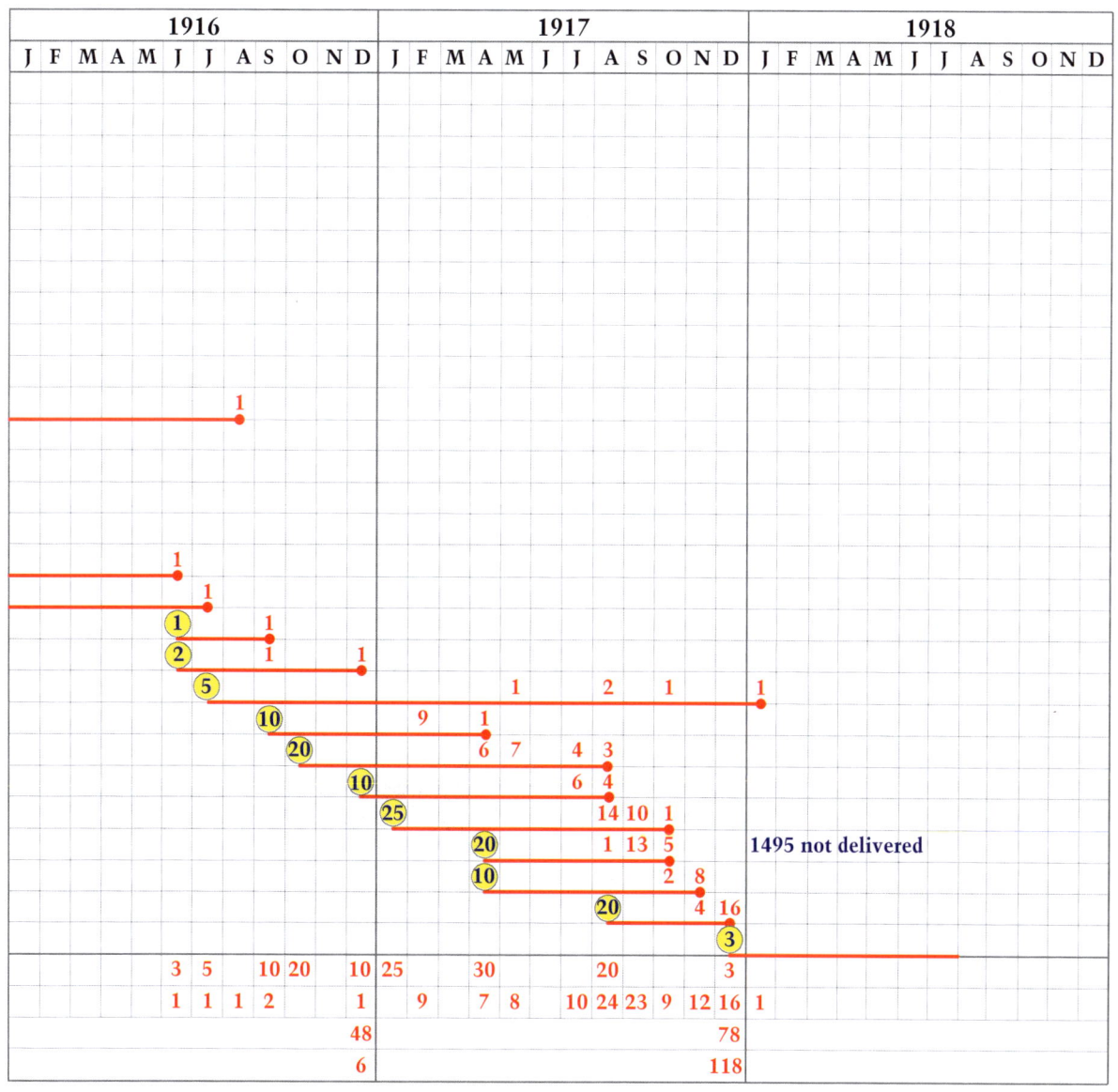

Albatros WDD & W.1

Above: Originally known as the Albatros WDD (for *Wasser Doppeldecker Doppelsitzer*, water biplane two-seater), the WDD and its modifications were retroactively designated Albatros W.1. The WDD first flew in the autumn of 1913.

The Albatros WDD (*Wasser Doppeldecker Doppelsitzer*; water biplane two-seater) first flew in autumn 1913 and was the naval version of the Albatros biplanes that would be classified as B.I in army service. The WDD was a three-bay biplane with two main floats and a tail float. The first WDD was powered by a 100 hp Argus engine; later versions had the 125 hp Argus or contemporary Mercedes or Benz engines. Early aircraft used brow radiators, but later aircraft used side radiators for cooling.

After some success in the 1913 Bodensee Contest the Navy ordered additional aircraft. These became Marine Numbers 52–56.

MN	Type	Engine
52	Albatros	Benz Bz.III
53	Albatros WDD	Mercedes
54	Albatros WDD	200 Argus
55	Albatros WDD	Mercedes
56	Albatros WDD	Benz Bz.III

Like many early aircraft, the WDD experienced running changes in production with little or no documentation about these changes surviving. These aircraft differed enough that had they been built later, at a time when designations were more formal and precise, they could have been given different designations. Changes in the vertical tail design and rear float were the most obvious of the changes made; other changes included the engine, radiators, and main floats..

The WDD and W.1 are covered here in the same section because the W.1 designation was apparently applied retroactively to several developments of the Albatros WDD. Marine Number 52 is an example. Part of the WDD series noted above, it is shown as a W.1 in various references – painted with Marine Number 552, allegedly to deceive Allied intelligence. The other WDD's in the series also were painted with a '5' preceding their actual Marine Number.

Marine Number 74 was another Albatros seaplane retroactively designated W.1, and others so redesignated are Marine Numbers 111, 221–230, 432, and 446.

Above: The Albatros WDD that competed in the 1913 Bodensee Contest had a smaller rudder than later aircraft.

			Albatros Seaplane Specifications				
Type	W.1	W.2	W.3	W.4 MN747	W.4 (948–967)	W.5	W.8
Engine	150 hp Benz Bz.III or 160 hp Mercedes D.III	150 hp Benz Bz.III	2x150 hp Benz Bz.III	160 hp Mercedes D.III	160 hp Mercedes D.III	2x150 hp Benz Bz.III	195 hp Benz Bz.IIIb
Span	14.3 m	10.0 m	22.7 m	9.50 m	9.50 m	22.7 m	11.46 m
Length	8.56 m	8.2 m	13.1 m	8.50 m	8.50 m	13.1 m	9.59 m
Wing Area	43.0 m²	31.4 m²	—	31.0 m²	—	100 m²	—
Empty Weight	—	935 kg.	—	709 kg	784 kg	2,263 kg	—
Flying Weight	—	1,215 kg	—	989 kg	155 km/h	3,665 kg	—
Maximum Speed	—	176 km/h	133 km/h	155 km/h	160 km/h	133 km/h	150 km/h
Climb to 1,000m	—	—	—	—	5.5 min.	20.0 min.	6.5 min.
Climb to 2,000m	—	—	—	—	8.5 min.	—	—
Climb to 3,000m	—	—	—	—	23 min.	—	34 min.
Duration	—	—	—	—	—	4 hours	3.5 hours
Guns	None	1 gun	1 gun	1 gun	2 guns	1 gun	1–2 fixed guns + 1 flexible gun

Above & Below: Side view of the Albatros WDD flown in the 1913 Bodensee Contest shows the rudder shape more clearly. (Peter M. Grosz Collection/SDTB)

Above & Below: These photos show the next evolution of the Albatros WDD design with a revised rudder shape and larger tail float. The seaplane below carries an early national insignia. (Peter M. Grosz Collection/SDTB)

Above: Marine Number 552 is a confusing aircraft. MN552 is identified as a Brandenburg built by Danzig in the list of marine numbers but is actually Albatros W.1 Marine Number 52. The Marine Numbers of Albatros W.I/WDD 52–56 were apparently prefixed with a '5' when painted to confuse Allied intelligence. However that worked, it did serve to confuse the author for a time! The W.1 has a redesigned tail compared to the WDD; the rudder was enlarged and the tail float was eliminated.

Below: This appears to be a front view of W.1 Marine Number 552. It has 3-bays of struts, is in similar pose as the other two photos, and has the navy ID pennants. The gravity tank under the upper wing is also present in all photos.

Above: Another view of Marine Number 552, identified as a Brandenburg built by Danzig in the list of marine numbers.
Below: Closeup of an Albatros W.I. (Peter M. Grosz Collection/SDTB)

Above: This Albatros WDD with enlarged tail surfaces and tail float retains the brow radiator. (Peter M. Grosz Collection/SDTB)
Below: Early Albatros WDD with brow radiator. (Peter M. Grosz Collection/SDTB)

Above: Later production Albatros WDD with side radiators and enlarged tail surfaces with horn-balanced rudder and tail float.

Above: Albatros WDD with side radiators and enlarged tail surfaces and tail float but no horn balance on rudder.

Above: This Albatros W.1 is seen just after take-off; it has no tail float but does have a leading edge radiator and carries national insignia and a naval pennant. (Peter M. Grosz Collection/SDTB)

Below: Early Albatros WDD Marine Number 20. (Peter M. Grosz Collection/SDTB)

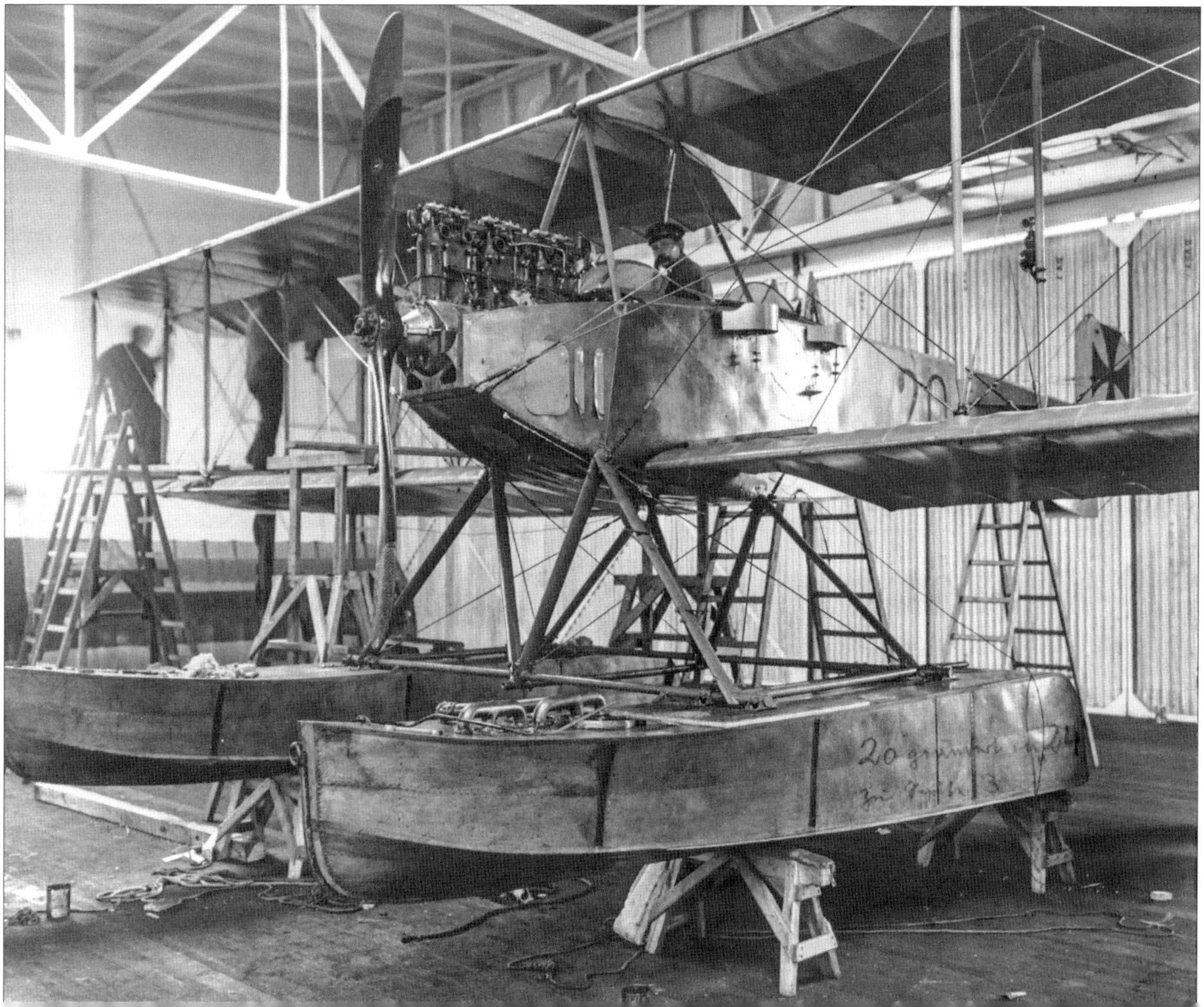

Above: This Albatros W.1 in its hangar has a later design of enlarged vertical tail surfaces without tail float. (Peter M. Bowers Collection/Museum of Flight)

Above: Beached Albatros W.1.

Above: Albatros W.1 Marine Number 55 was assigned to the Kiel naval air station. It has side radiators and tail float and the main floats are of revised design. The wings have been roughly cropped; likely as a result of a forced landing at sea with the crew chopping off the outer wings to make the aircraft more stable on the water while awaiting rescue. (Peter M. Grosz Collection/SDTB)

Below: Albatros W.1 Marine Number 74 was assigned to the Kiel naval air station. It has side radiators and tail float and the main floats are of original design. It carries 1918 national insignia on its rudder and naval pennants. The engine exhaust manifolds and float design differ from those shown on the facing page on this same aircraft. (Peter M. Grosz Collection/SDTB)

Above & Below: Albatros W.1 Marine Number 74 was assigned to the Kiel naval air station. It has side radiators and tail float although the main floats are of revised design. It carries 1918 national insignia on its rudder and a naval pennant. (Peter M. Grosz Collection/SDTB)

Above: Albatros W.1 Marine Number 223 being hoisted out of the water after an accident. (Peter M. Grosz Collection/SDTB)

Facing Page: Albatros W.1 Marine Number 228 (top) and W.1 Marine Number 229 (bottom) illustrate the final configuration of the Albatros W.1 with enlarged tail surfaces and no tail float. (Peter M. Grosz Collection/SDTB)

Below: Albatros W.1 Marine Number 226 appears to be a total loss. Marine Number 512 in the background is a Brandenburg FB. (Peter M. Grosz Collection/SDTB)

Above: Albatros W.1 Marine Number 229 being brought ashore after a flight. (Peter M. Grosz Collection/SDTB)
Below: Albatros W.1 Marine Number 230 afloat before a flight. (Peter M. Grosz Collection/SDTB)

Above: Late production Albatros W.1 ready for take-off. (Peter M. Bowers Collection/Museum of Flight)
Below: Late production Albatros W.1 taking off.

Albatros W.2

Above: The sole example of the Albatros W.2 is shown before its Marine Number of 450 was applied. The engine was a 160 hp Mercedes D.III.

The Albatros W.2 was a reconnaissance floatplane derived from the C.III airframe. Powered by a 160 hp Mercedes D.III engine, the W.2 had a flexible gun for the observer; unlike the C.III, the pilot did not have a fixed gun. A single W.2, Marine Number 450, was ordered in December 1915 and delivered in June 1916. No further production was undertaken and no details are available.

The W.2 was a clean-looking design derived from a successful land reconnaissance type, so would seem to be a serious candidate for production. Perhaps its simple float undercarriage was not robust enough compared to its Friedrichshafen counterparts.

Above: The last of three logos used by the Axial propeller is also the most well known. The first logo was a dagger with the name "Axial" on the blade.

Above & Below: The Albatros W.2 was a clean design for a two-seat reconnaissance floatplane. The observer had a single flexible machine gun; there was no fixed gun for the pilot.

Albatros W.3

Above: Marine Number 527 was the only Albatros W.3 built. The W.3 was a class TMG, a torpedo bomber armed with two flexible machine guns.

The Albatros W.3 was ordered in October 1915 and delivered in July 1916. It was the first torpedo bomber built by Albatros and only a single prototype, Marine Number 527, was built.

The W.3 was a twin-engine floatplane with its two 150 hp Benz Bz.III engines mounted as pushers. To improve streamlining the pusher propellers had spinners. The large, boxy radiators were mounted at the top front of the nacelles. The wood structure was typical of Albatros practice of the time and the design had typical Albatros lines. The design provided for a torpedo carried under the fuselage and semi-recessed to reduce drag.

Little is known about the W.3's handling qualities, but the overall design was worthy of development into the very similar Albatros W.5 that was essentially the production version of the W.3 prototype.

Facing Page: Two views of the Albatros W.3 under construction at the factory. The W.3 had ailerons on the upper wing only and used typical Albatros wood construction. (Peter M. Bowers Collection, Museum of Flight)

Right: Photograph of the Anker-Propeller logo.

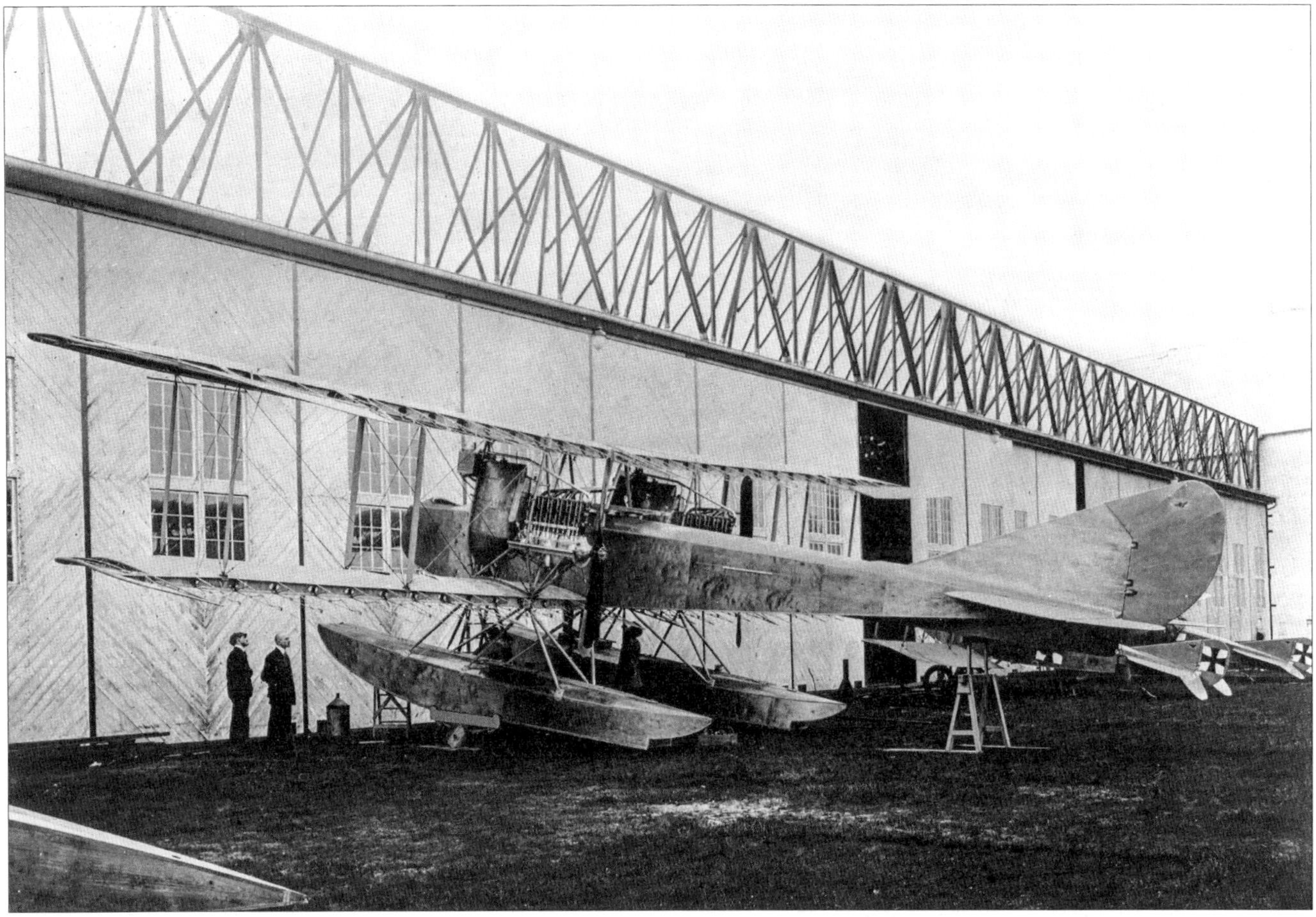

85

Above & Below: The completed Albatros W.3 was a clean design with minimal frontal area for a fairly large, twin-engine biplane floatplane. Albatros had learned the importance of streamlining for performance and applied that lesson to the W.3. (Peter M. Grosz Collection, SDTB)

Above & Below: These views of the completed Albatros W.3 emphasize the attention paid to streamlining this large biplane floatplane. The pusher propellers featured spinners and the large block radiators were carefully streamlined into the engine nacelles. (Peter M. Bowers Collection, Museum of Flight)

Albatros W.1 Marine Number 55 assigned to the Kiel Naval Air Station.

Albatros W.3 SVK Drawing

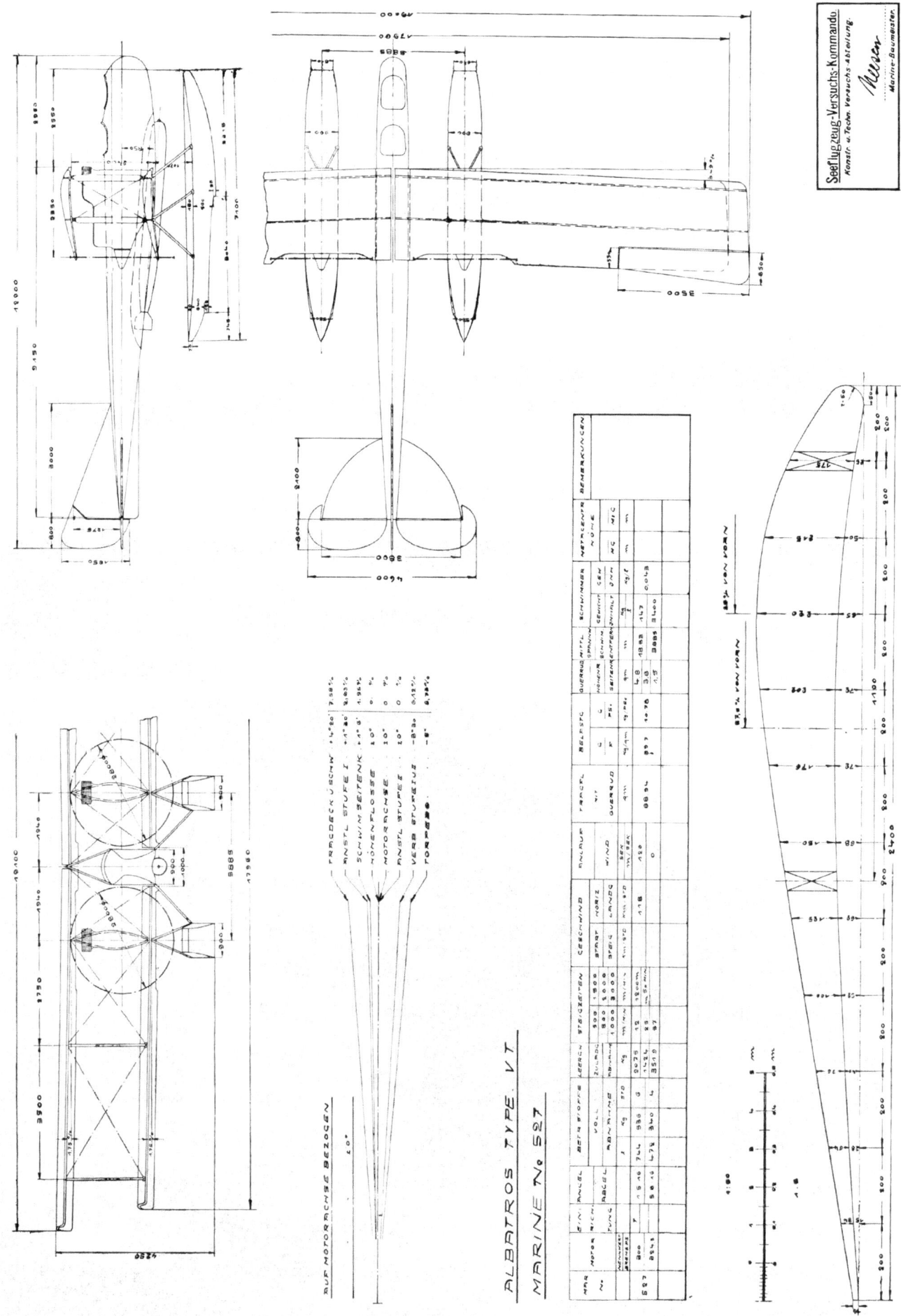

Albatros W.1 & W.4

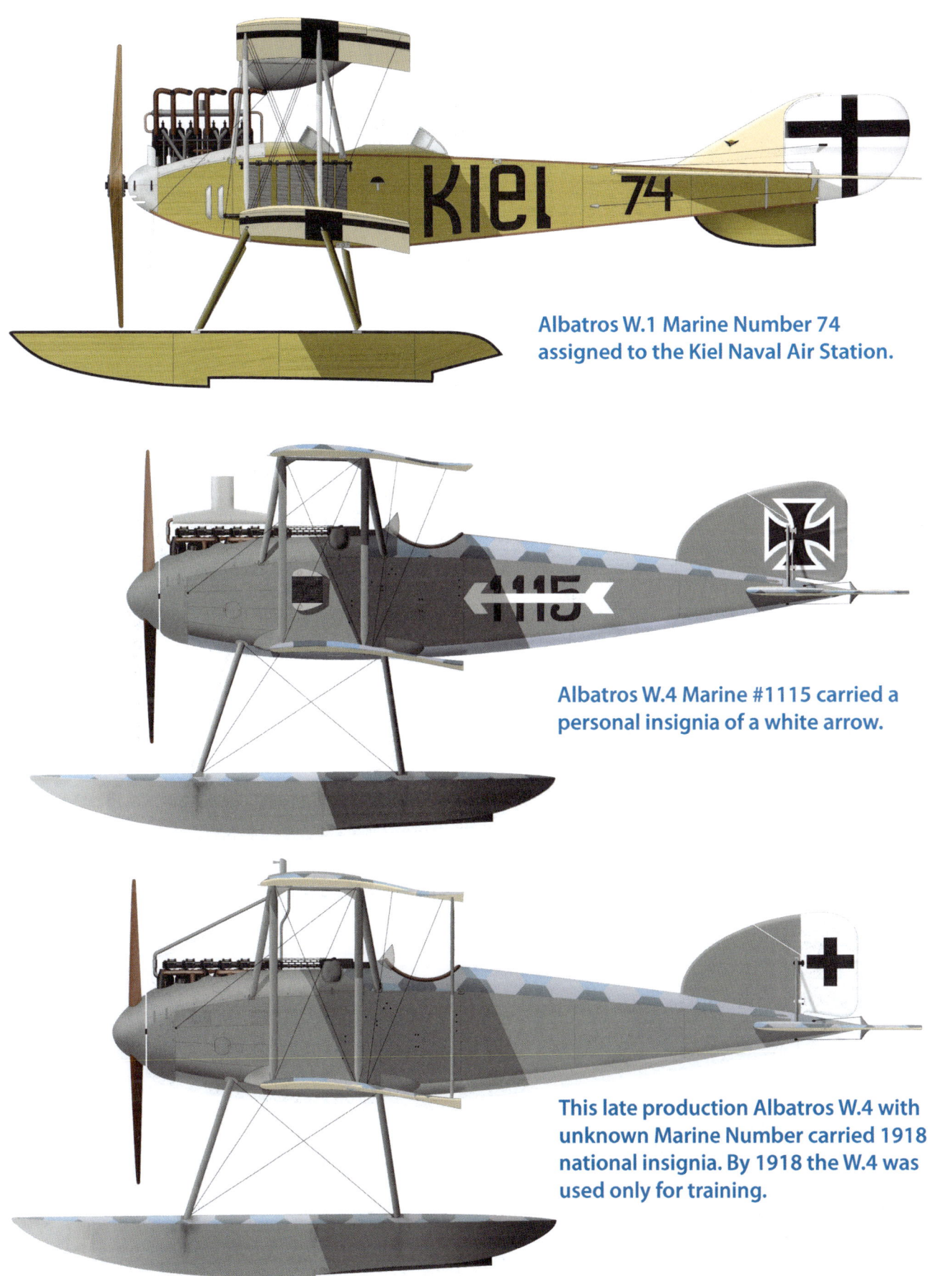

Albatros W.1 Marine Number 74 assigned to the Kiel Naval Air Station.

Albatros W.4 Marine #1115 carried a personal insignia of a white arrow.

This late production Albatros W.4 with unknown Marine Number carried 1918 national insignia. By 1918 the W.4 was used only for training.

Albatros W.4

Albatros, the largest WWI German aircraft manufacturer, responded to the Navy's request for a floatplane fighter with the W.4, a seaplane development of their Albatros D.I fighter that was being built at the same time. Both the W.4 and D.I were powered by the 160 hp Mercedes D.III engine. Due to its floats, the W.4 was heavier than the D.I and needed larger wings for more lift. The horizontal tail was larger to compensate for the larger wings, and flight testing of the prototype revealed tail heaviness. Changing the amount of stagger solved the problem and happily also improved climb rate and top speed. The prototype and initial production W.4s had ear radiators and a single machine gun. The harsh operating environment caused considerable problems with the wood floats and a number of different designs had to be tried both for strength and seaworthiness. Repairs and water-proofing the leading edge and spars of the lower wings were also required after water damage, including delamination of the spars, was discovered. Starting with the second W.4 production batch, two machine guns were fitted.

The arrival of summer weather revealed problems with the ear radiators, which had to be replaced with a new design. Starting with the fifth production batch (1484–1503), airfoil radiators were fitted to reduce drag. To improve maneuverability the last two production batches were fitted with ailerons on all four wings. A total of 118 W.4s were built.

By the time the final production batch was built, the Brandenburg W.12 two-seat floatplane fighter had proved it was more effective in combat than single-seater floatplane fighters and the final production batch of W.4s was delivered directly to storage. Eight W.4s were traded to the Austro-Hungarian Navy in July 1918 in return for Austro-Daimler V-12 engines to power Staaken R-planes. Designated E5 to E12 in Austro-Hungarian service, these saw no combat. By August 1918 only four W.4s were on combat duty on the North Sea and another five were on combat duty in Turkey.

Above: Albatros W.4 prototype MN 747 with visiting dignitaries in the background. Behind MN747 the tail of MN749 can be seen at left. MN749 was the Friedrichshafen FF43 that was a competitor for single-seat floatplane fighter orders from the Navy, but only one was built. Despite remaining a single prototype, the FF43 was assigned to Zeebrügge where it scored a victory. (Peter M. Bowers Collection/Museum of Flight)

Albatros W.4

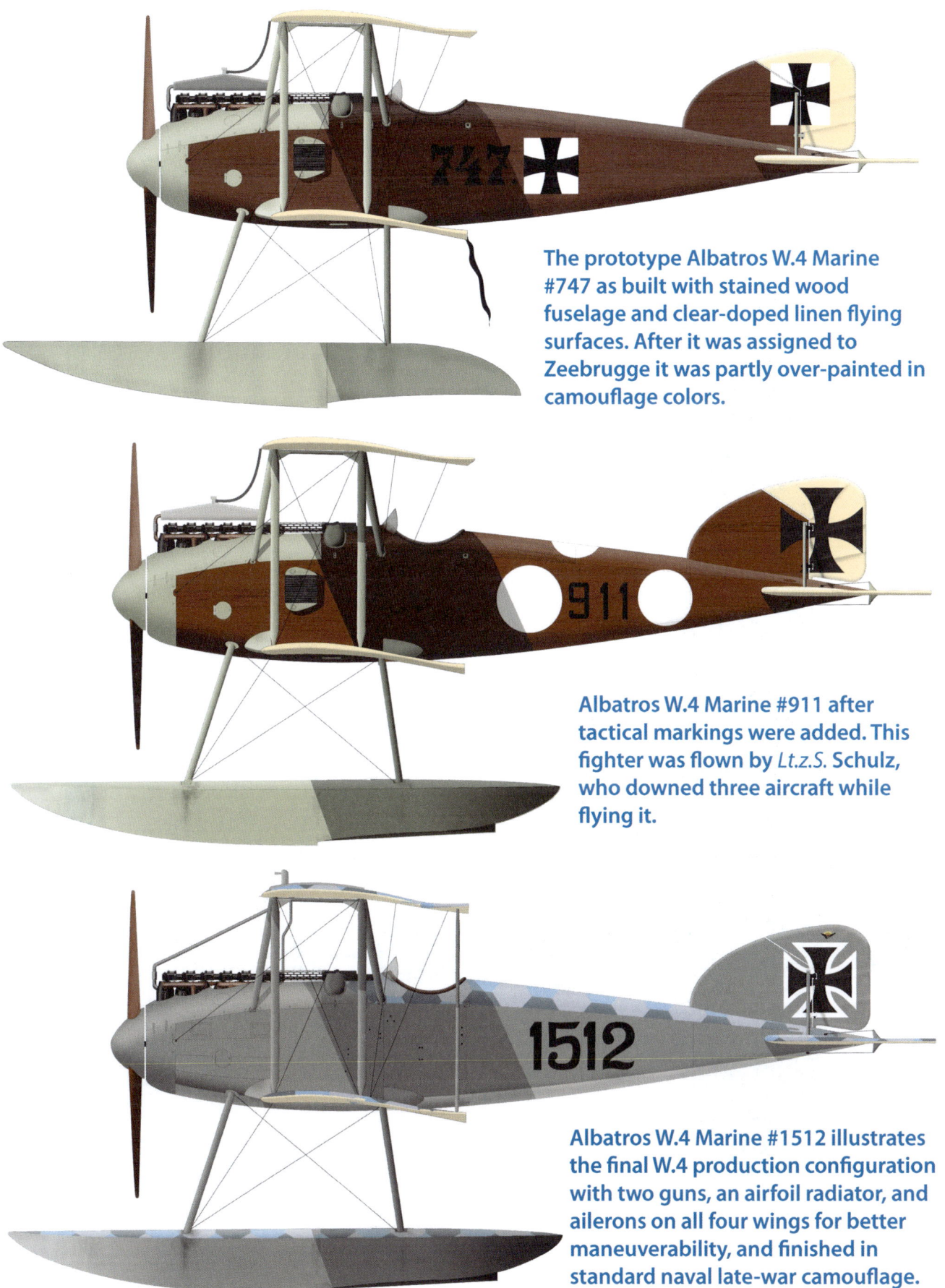

The prototype Albatros W.4 Marine #747 as built with stained wood fuselage and clear-doped linen flying surfaces. After it was assigned to Zeebrugge it was partly over-painted in camouflage colors.

Albatros W.4 Marine #911 after tactical markings were added. This fighter was flown by *Lt.z.S.* Schulz, who downed three aircraft while flying it.

Albatros W.4 Marine #1512 illustrates the final W.4 production configuration with two guns, an airfoil radiator, and ailerons on all four wings for better maneuverability, and finished in standard naval late-war camouflage.

Above: Seaplanes lined up at Windau in 1917 include at least seven Albatros W.4 fighters, with Marine Numbers 911, 958, and 1107 visible on the original photo. Albatros W.4 Marine #911 is the aircraft in the right background with the two circles on the fuselage. Marine #911 was the most successful Albatros W.4 in the Baltic; *Lt.z.S.* Schulz downed three aircraft while flying it. Friedrichshafen FF33L Marine #1263, a category CHFT reconnaissance two-seater, is in the left foreground, and a similar machine is at right.

Albatros W.4 Production Summary

Marine Number	Qty	Notes
747, 785–786	3	Prototypes; 1 gun, ear radiators
902–911	10	1 gun, ear radiators
948–967	20	2 guns, ear radiators
1107–1116	10	2 guns, ear radiators
1302–1326	25	2 guns, ear radiators
1484–1503	20	2 guns, airfoil radiator, 4 ailerons
1504–1513	10	2 guns, airfoil radiator, 4 ailerons
1719–1738	20	As 1504–1513; delivered directly to storage.

A total of 118 W.4 fighters were built in a series of production batches summarized in this table.

Above: Albatros W.4 prototype Marine Number 747.

Above: Albatros W.4 Marine #964 of the second production batch. (Peter M. Grosz Collection/SDTB)

Right: This view of wrecked Albatros W.4 Marine #958 of the second production batch being recovered from the water shows the three-color naval hexagonal camouflage fabric used on later production aircraft. The printed fabric was used on all upper surfaces. Printing the color on the fabric during manufacture saved time, labor, the weight of paint, and the paint itself.

Above: Albatros W.4 Marine #965 outside its hangar. The dent in the spinner appears to match the two photos opposite.

Above: Albatros W.4 #956 of the second production batch. The ear radiator is prominent and, located on both sides of the aircraft, partially spoiled the clean aerodynamic lines of the fuselage. This was addressed by using lower-drag airfoil radiators in the last three production batches.

Above: Albatros W.4 Marine #965, an aircraft of the second production batch, with its pilot.

Below: The above photo seems to have been retouched to show a woman in the cockpit. The photo is in 'pin-up' style, perhaps for a postcard. The dent in the spinner appears to be the same in both photos.

Above: Albatros W.4 Marine #1318, from the fourth production batch, is shown here at the Austro-Hungarian *Seeflugstation Puntisella* in July 1918 before its new Austro-Hungarian serial E12 was applied.

Below: Albatros W.4 Marine #1322 from the fourth production batch has been damaged by a hard landing. It wears the late insignia so this photo is from 1918, indicating training use. (Peter M. Grosz Collection/SDTB)

Above: With airfoil radiator, four ailerons, and two guns, MN1486 is in the final W.4 production configuration. (Peter M. Bowers Collection/Museum of Flight)

Right: W.4 MN1486 having a bad day.

Below: Albatros W.4 MN1322 in flight.

Above: Early Albatros W.4 with ear radiators. (Peter M. Bowers Collection/Museum of Flight)
Below: W.4 MN1495 of the 5th production batch undergoing factory stress testing.

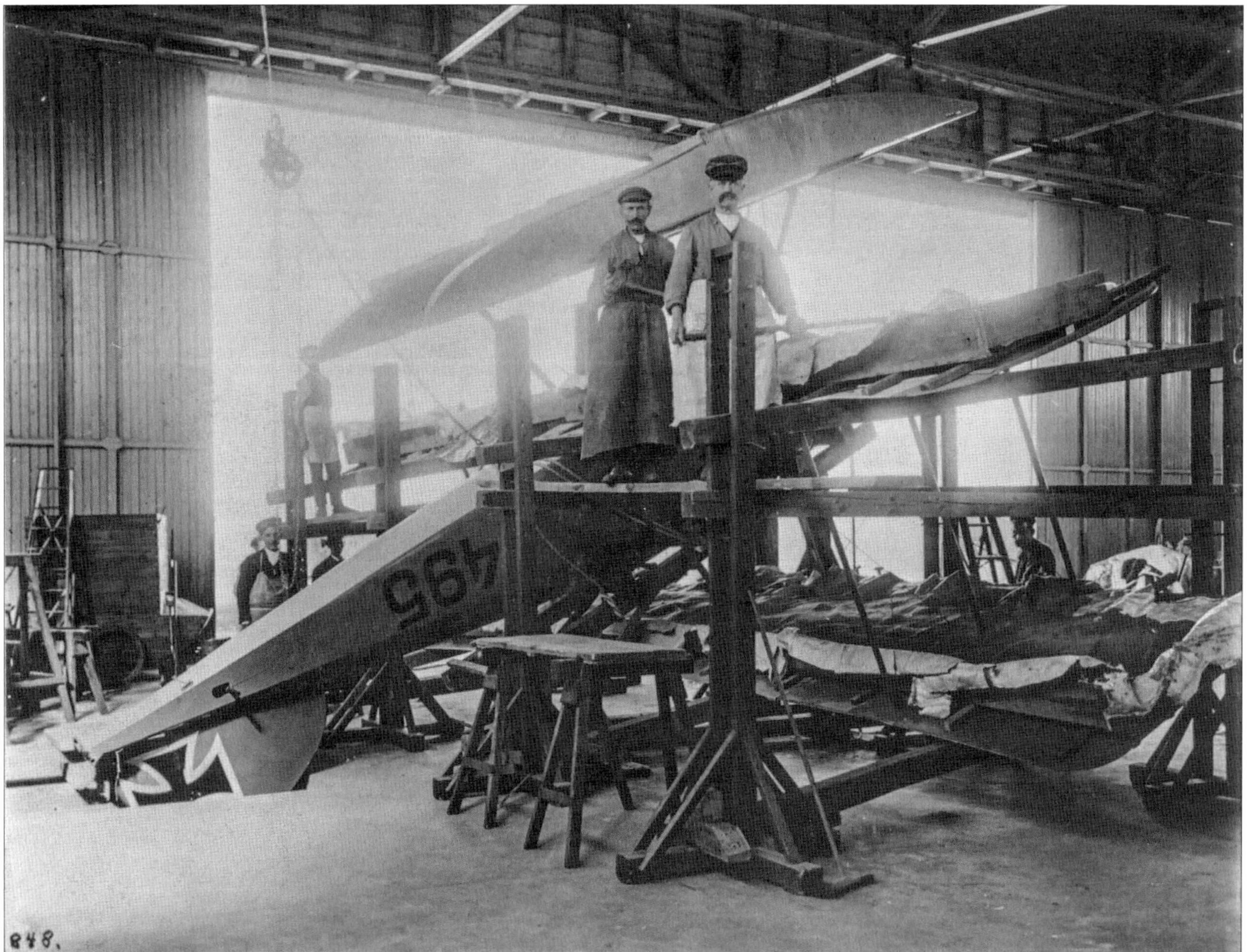

Above: Albatros W.4 Marine #954, from the third production batch. (Peter M. Grosz Collection/SDTB)
Below: Early production Albatros W.4 being hoisted out of the water. (Peter M. Grosz Collection/SDTB)

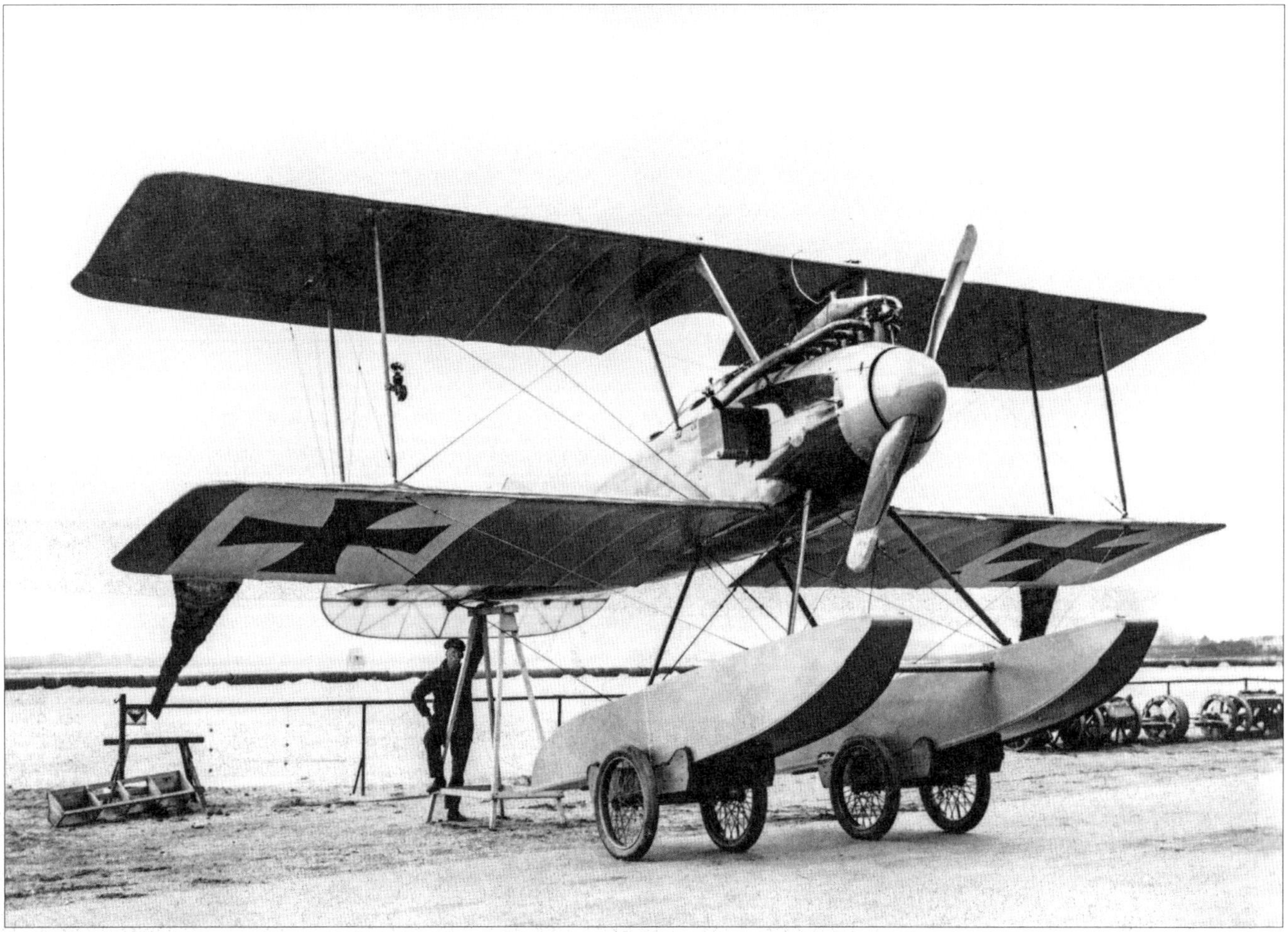

Above: Early production Albatros W.4 on beaching trolleys. (Peter M. Grosz Collection/SDTB)

Below: Late production Albatros W.4 with four ailerons and 1918 insignia. (Peter M. Grosz Collection/SDTB)

Above & Below: W.4 MN1512, sixth production batch, illustrates the final production configuration of four ailerons, an airfoil radiator, and the late naval camouflage scheme. (Above: Peter M. Bowers Collection/Museum of Flight)

Above: W.4 MN1512 illustrates the final production configuration of four ailerons, an airfoil radiator, and the late naval camouflage scheme. (Peter M. Grosz Collection/SDTB)

Above: Albatros W.4 Marine Number 911, last aircraft of the first production batch, is nearest the camera. W.4 #911 later had additional tactical markings added as illustrated in the profile on page 91.

Above: Albatros W.4 MN 1115 of the third production batch carries an arrow as a personal insignia; the pilot looks pleased to be photographed with his fighter.

Above: A crane rescues an Albatros W.4 having a bad day; the naval camouflage fabric is well shown. (Courtesy Bruno Schmäling)

Albatros W.4 SVK Drawing, MN 747, 785, 786

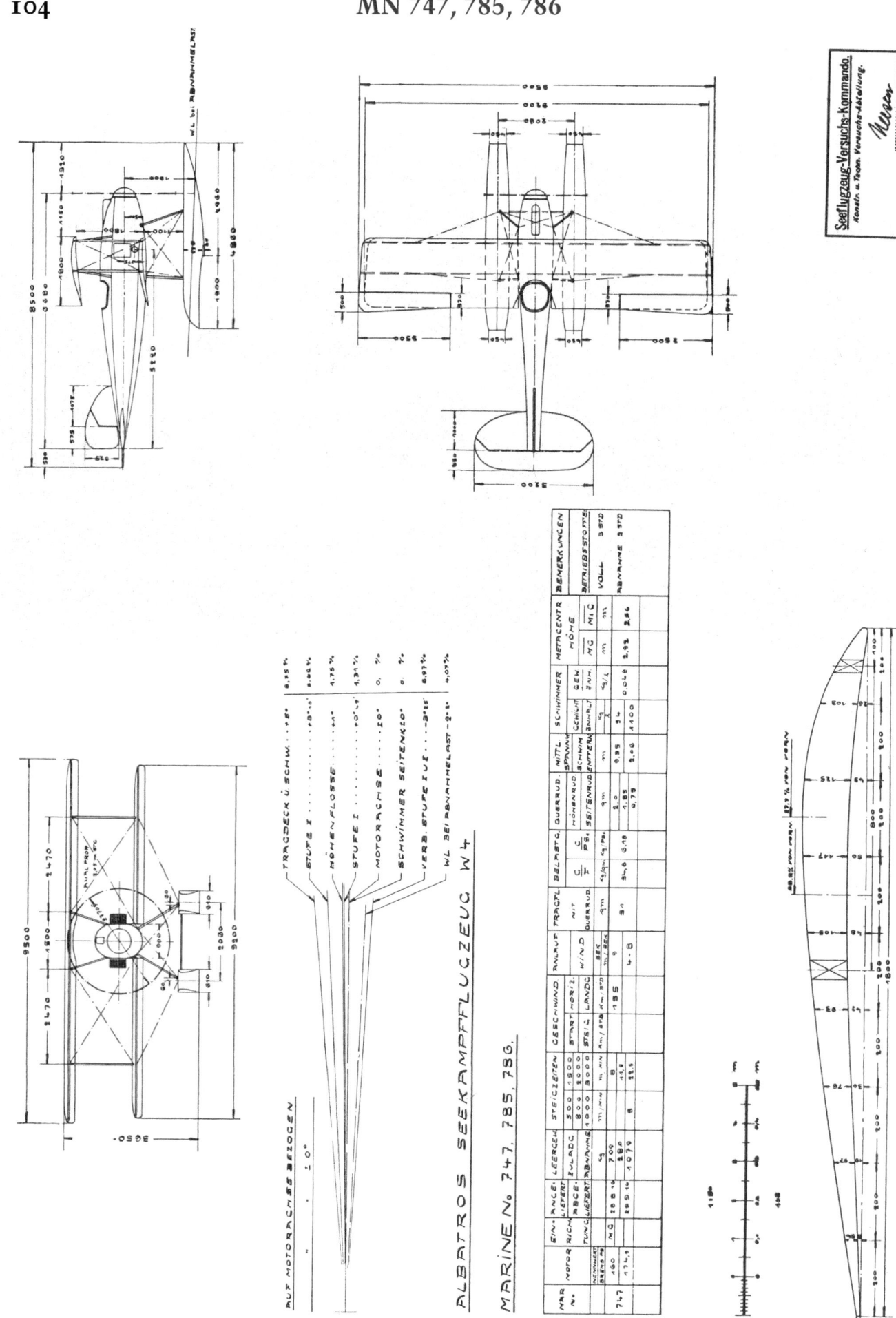

Albatros W.4 SVK Drawing, MN 902–911

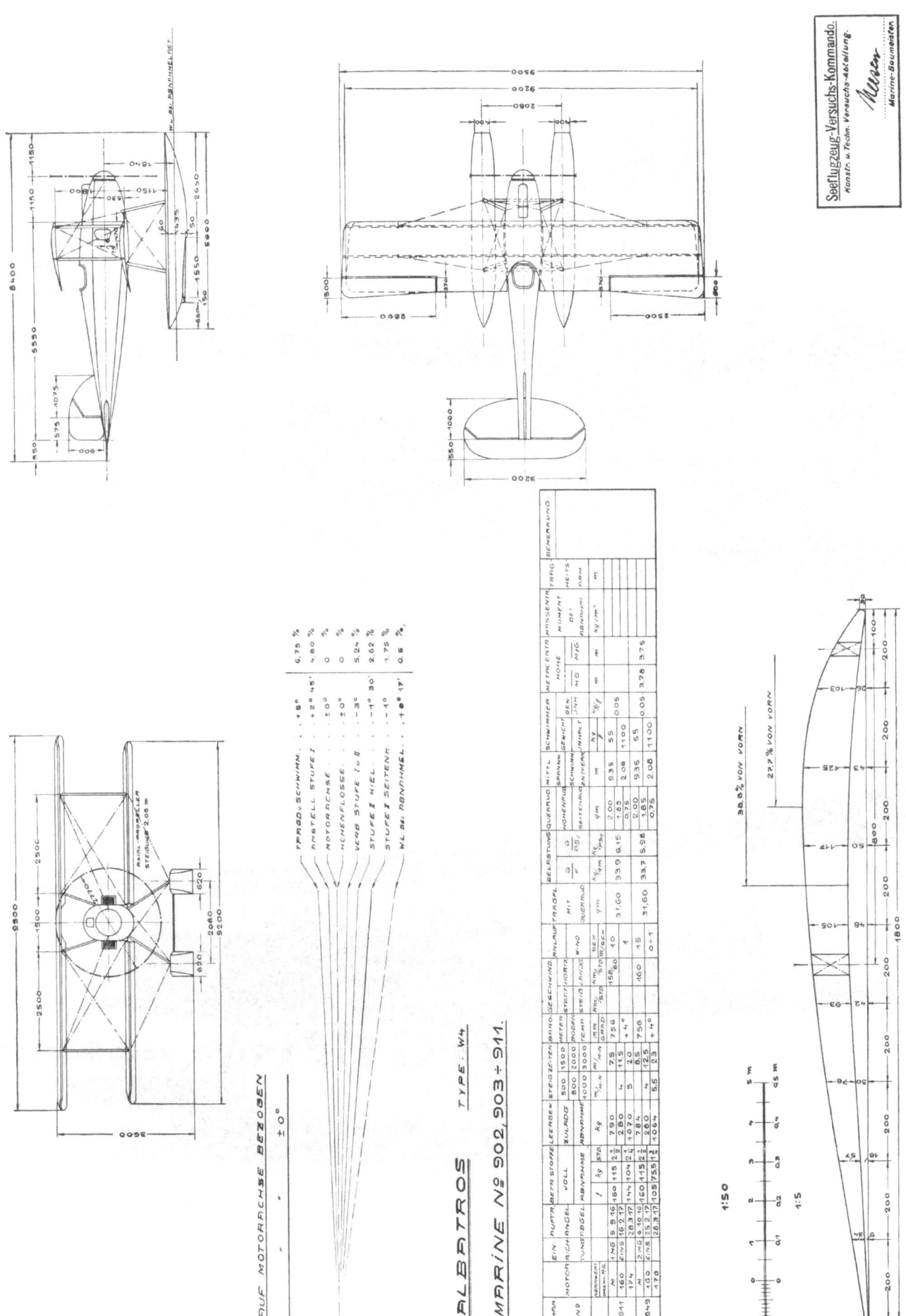

Albatros W.5

Above: The single Albatros W.3 prototype was followed by a batch of five W.5 production aircraft. The W.5 was developed from the W.3 and like the W.3 was a class TMG, a torpedo bomber armed with two flexible machine guns. Above Marine Number 845, the first aircraft of the batch, launches a torpedo.

A batch of five Albatros W.5 torpedo bombers, Marine Numbers 845–849, was ordered in July 1916, the same month the W.3 was delivered. Apparently the priority of the W.5 was fairly low as deliveries of the five aircraft were stretched out from May 1917 to January 1918.

The W.5 was essential a refined derivative of the original W.3 and shared many similarities with the earlier design. Wing span and length of the W.3 and W.5 were the same and both types were powered by two 150 hp Benz Bz.III engines mounted as pushers. Like the W.3, the W.5 had propeller spinners and provision for a single torpedo mounted below the fuselage, although the torpedo recess under the fuselage was larger in the W.5. The radiators and engine nacelles of the W.5 were more refined for lower drag with better cooling. Photos of Marine Number 845 show ailerons on the upper wing only like the W.3, but apparently lateral control needed improvement because Marine Number 847 had ailerons on all four wings connected by an actuating strut. The SVK drawing of the W.5, which indicated it applied to all five Marine Numbers built, show ailerons on all four wings, so that was intended as the standard configuration. It is not known if MN 845 was later modified to have four ailerons or left in its original configuration. The floats of the W.5 were enlarged compared to the W.3.

The small production order is an indication that the W.5's performance was below that of its Gotha and Brandenburg competitors, and the leisurely delivery schedule reflects the low priority given torpedo bombers after the Navy abandoned aerial torpedo attacks due to the vulnerability of the attacking aircraft.

Above: Marine Number 845 was the first of five W.5 ordered. The photo shows that ailerons were fitted to the upper wing only, while the SVK drawing shows ailerons were to be fitted to all four wings. The rudder has a curved trailing edge; later aircraft and the SVK drawing feature a rudder with straight trailing edge.

Above: This view of Marine Number 845 also shows that ailerons were fitted to the upper wing only on this aircraft. It is not known if this aircraft was later upgraded to the standard four-aileron configuration shown in the SVK drawing.

Above: Marine Number 847 was the third of five W.5 ordered. The photo shows that ailerons were fitted to all four wings, which is consistent with the type's SVK drawing. Four ailerons was intended as the standard configuration. A torpedo has been loaded and the torpedo's nose and fins are visible. (Peter M. Bowers Collection/Museum of Flight)

German Torpedo Bomber Production					
Type	Albatros W.5	Gotha WD11	Gotha WD14	Brandenburg GW	Friedrichshafen FF41AT
Number	5	17	52*	21	8

* 69 ordered, production was curtailed by the Armistice.
There were a number of prototype torpedo bombers; this table shows only production types. The Albatros W.5 was produced in the smallest quantity of any production type, an indication of its relative merit. The Gotha WD14 received by far the largest orders. It was also the only aircraft in the table powered by 200 hp Benz Bz.IV engines; the others were all underpowered by 150 hp Benz Bz.III engines.

Above: This view of W.5 Marine Number 847 was likely taken at the same time as the photos above because the torpedo fins are still visible beloew the fuselage. The rudder has a straight trailing edge. (Peter M. Bowers Collection/Museum of Flight)

Albatros W.5 SVK Drawing

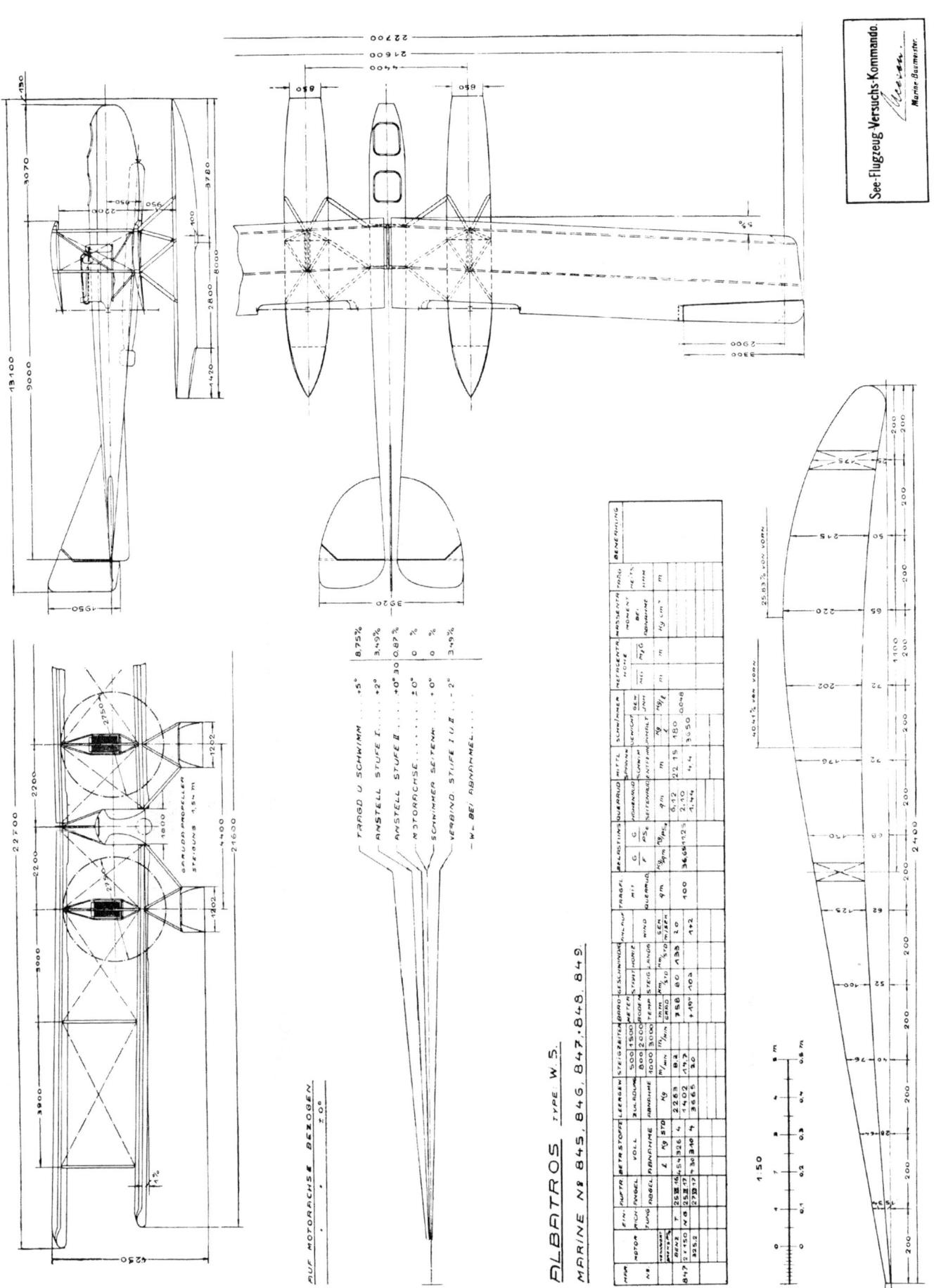

Above: Quarter view of a W.5 in the final configuration with ailerons on all four wings connected by an actuating strut. (Peter M. Bowers Collection/Museum of Flight)

Above: Front view of a W.5 in the early configuration with ailerons on the upper wing only. No torpedo is being carried. (Peter M. Bowers Collection/Museum of Flight)

Below: Front view of a W.5 in the final configuration with ailerons on all four wings connected by an actuating strut. In this view a torpedo is being carried. (Peter M. Bowers Collection/Museum of Flight)

Albatros W.5

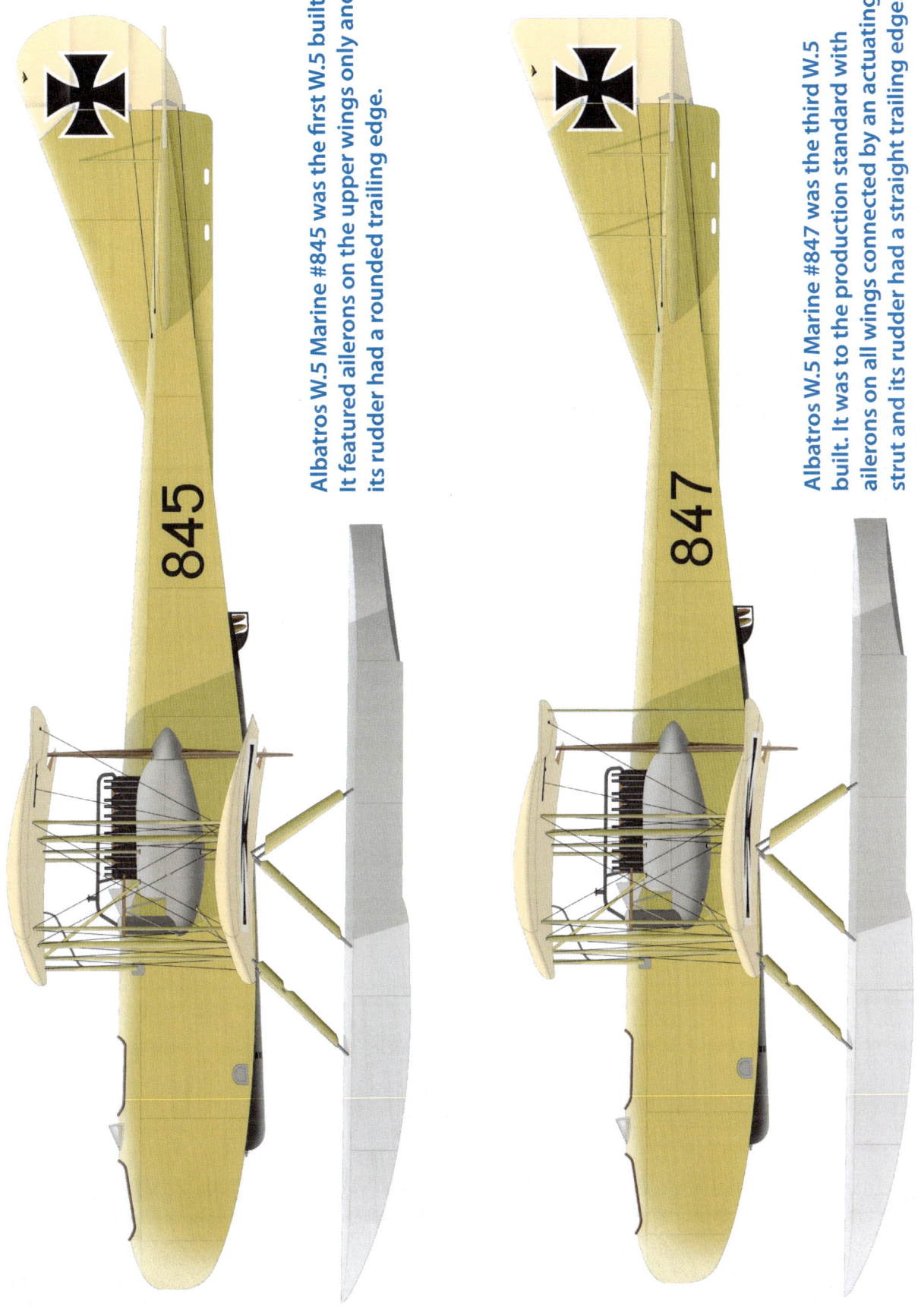

Albatros W.5 Marine #845 was the first W.5 built. It featured ailerons on the upper wings only and its rudder had a rounded trailing edge.

Albatros W.5 Marine #847 was the third W.5 built. It was to the production standard with ailerons on all wings connected by an actuating strut and its rudder had a straight trailing edge.

Albatros W.8

Above: The first prototype Albatros W8 was a handsome, well-streamlined two-seat fighter powered by a V-8 that was not yet in mass production. However, the flat radiator under the wing somewhat spoiled the overall streamlining.

The Albatros W.6 and W.7 designs were not built, making the Albatros W.8 the last wartime Albatros seaplane. The company offered the Albatros W.8 to the Navy's to satisfy its two-seat floatplane fighter needs. Although similar in concept to the Brandenburg W.12, its tail design obstructed more of the gunner's field of fire and it used an experimental engine, the 195 hp Benz Bz.IIIb, that reached production too late to power aircraft at the front. Moreover, despite the power of its V8 engine, it was slower than the W.12 biplane, and the W.29 monoplane was faster yet. By the time the Albatros W.8 was tested, the superior Brandenburg W.29 monoplane was already in service. Only three aircraft, Marine Numbers 5001–5003, were ordered and it is not certain that MN5003 was completed.

Above & Below: Two views of Marine #5002, the second Albatros W8 prototype, shows that the elegant spinner of the prototype was abandoned. Otherwise #5502 appears to incorporate no other visible changes. The block radiator beneath the upper wing undoubtedly produced a lot of drag, and one wonders if it was intended for use in production aircraft if any had been ordered. A nose radiator seems better suited to minimize cooling drag. (Peter M. Bowers Collection/Museum of Flight)

Above & Below: Two additional views of Marine Number 5002, the second Albatros W.8 prototype. Despite elimination of the elegant spinner of the first prototype, the W.8 had clean lines and small frontal area marred only by the bulky block radiator beneath the upper wing. (Peter M. Bowers Collection/Museum of Flight)

Albatros Miscellaneous L-Types

After WWI was over, Albatros, a major aircraft manufacturer in defeated Germany, decided to retroactively introduce a designation system for their aircraft and projects that had nothing to do with military type designations. The result was the Albatros L Designations that were applied arbitrarily. The L designations were neither chronological nor did they link aircraft in a design lineage. The complete list is given on page 7 of volume 1.

At least two of these aircraft were not given formal military designations, nor were they produced in quantity or used operationally. These two aircraft, the L3 and the L9, are presented here for completeness.

Albatros L3

Above: Known as the GDD 100 hp Gnome, the L3 was a small single-seat biplane. It was probably built in 1914 or early 1915 and was powered by a 100 hp Gnôme rotary. It was likely intended as a scout (reconnaissance) aircraft; however, the German Army preferred two-seat reconnaissance aircraft. Construction appears to consist of a semi-monocoque plywood fuselage and conventional wood, wire, and fabric wings, all of which was typical of standard Albatros practice. (Peter M. Bowers Collection/Museum of Flight)

Albatros L9

Above: The Albatros L9, designed by Dorner, had thick, high-lift wings similar to the later Albatros G.III bomber. The wings were greatly staggered and a small, vulnerable-looking button rudder without fixed fin was used. Power was from a 100 hp Albatros D.I engine with brow radiator mounted over the engine. Directional stability would seem to have been marginal. A single interplane strut was used together with large struts bracing the wing spars. Despite the eccentric configuration, this aircraft may have been an ancestor of the later Albatros fighters. (Peter M. Bowers Collection/Museum of Flight)

Albatros L Designations

L #	Military Designation	L #	Military Designation	L #	Military Designation
L1	B.I	L17	D.II	L33	C.Ib
L2	B.II	L18	C.VII	L34	D.VII
L3	GDD 100 hp Gnome	L19	C.VIII	L35	D.VIII (project)
L4	G.I (OAW)	L20	D.III	L36	Dr.I
L5	B.III	L21	G.III	L37	D.IX
L6	C.I	L22	D.IV	L38	D.X
L7	C.I (OAW)	L23	C.IX	L39	Dr.II
L8	C.II	L24	D.V/Va	L40	J.I
L9	ME	L25	C.X	L41	D.XI
L10	C.III	L26	C.XI	L42	J.II
L11	G.II	L27	C.XII	L43	D.XII
L12	C.IV	L28	D.VI (projected pusher)	L44	D.XIII (not completed)
L13	C.II (OAW)	L29	C.XIII	L45	D.XIIIa (not completed)
L14	C.V	L30	B.IIa	L46	D.XIV (not completed)
L15	D.I	L31	C.XIV	L47	C.XV
L16	C.VI	L32	C.Ia		

Above & Below: Two more views of the unusual Albatros L9 are shown here. The interplane struts, which connect the rear spar of the top wing to the front spar of the bottom wing, seem inadequate and may indicate the wings were essentially cantilever designs. The interplane strut improved aileron effectiveness by stiffening the wing cellule.

Facing Page: The table lists the L designation for all wartime Albatros designs. The three types denoted (OAW) were originally designated OAW G.I, OAW C.I and OAW C.II. At the time these aircraft were built the license manufacturer designation, in this case (OAW), had not yet been introduced. OAW was a wholly-owned Albatros subsidiary.

Albatros Bombers, Seaplanes, and J-Types in Retrospect

Albatros was the largest manufacturer of warplanes in WWI Germany; as such, it had significant advantages over competing firms. One advantage was its large production capacity that enabled it to rapidly produce aircraft of conventional wood, wire, and fabric construction. A more unfair advantage was its close ties with ranking Army officers who were responsible for purchasing aircraft for the Army. Despite those advantages, Albatros had only limited success designing and manufacturing the armored J-types, bombers, and seaplanes covered in this volume.

Albatros developed its aircraft in a series of evolutionary steps based on a consistent and conventional structural technology using semi-monocoque plywood fuselages and typical wood, wire, and fabric wings. This approach served Albatros well from the first unarmed two-seater, the B.I, through the more powerful and streamlined second-generation C.VII and D.I of mid-1916. The intervening two-seater types were all solid, reliable performers that performed well on operations.

Albatros continued this workman-like progression with both its fighters and two-seaters throughout the war, and applied the same approach to its bombers, seaplanes, and J-types. Albatros was generally successful with fighters and two-seat reconnaissance planes until the early summer of 1917 when the new generation of Allied fighters arrived at the front in numbers. At this time the steady, evolutionary Albatros design approach faltered and innovation in structures and aerodynamics was needed to produce superior warplanes.

When *Idflieg* ordered J-type armored infantry aircraft from the aircraft industry, Albatros naturally responded and created their J.I from the mediocre C.XII reconnaissance plane. The Albatros J.I was the only J-type without engine armor, and consequently was the least successful J-type. The Albatros J.II rectified that short-coming with a fully-armored engine, so was more successful. However, despite the massive Albatros production capacity, fewer Albatros J-types were ordered than from either competitor, AEG or Junkers. The reason is not difficult to determine; both the AEG and Junkers J-types used metal airframes that were much more resistant to ground fire than the wooden airframes of the Albatros J-types. Moreover, all J-types were limited to the 200/220 hp Benz Bz.IV/IVa, which limited performance and compromised maneuverability and safety of flight. The 260 hp Mercedes D.IVa that should have been used was not made available, although that engine was essentially wasted on production of the mediocre C.X and C.XII.

Albatros's foray into bomber design and production was even less successful. A small batch of Albatros G.III bombers was built and used at the front, but there were no repeat orders nor further development. AEG, Friedrichshafen, and Gotha built better bombers and Albatros exited that business.

Albatros had built a limited number of seaplanes before the war and small numbers of unarmed two-seaters were purchased and used for training and reconnaissance. Competing seaplanes, especially those built by Friedrichshafen, proved more robust during operations and few Albatros reconnaissance seaplanes were built. Albatros also built a very few two-engine torpedo bomber seaplanes, but again competing companies built better aircraft and there were no further torpedo plane orders from Albatros.

Perhaps unsurprisingly, Albatros's one real success with seaplanes was their W.4, a floatplane development of the successful D.I Army fighter. Unfortunately, the German navy was only allowed to purchase about 5% of the number of Army airplanes so the total seaplane market was small. Furthermore, after some operational experience the German Navy realized that single-seat seaplane fighters could only undertake short-range defensive operations on behalf of naval air stations. The need to undertake longer-range offensive operations, especially against the powerful America and Felixstowe flying boats over the North Sea, demanded two-seat floatplane fighters, and Brandenburg fulfilled that requirement very successfully with its W.12/W.19/W.29 series. The Albatros W.8 competitor to the Brandenburg seaplane fighters was no improvement and was not produced in quantity.

Despite its huge production capacity, Albatros's design department could not keep up with the competition after mid-1917 even in its most successful product lines, fighters and C-type reconnaissance planes. Albatros's success in armored J-types, bombers, and seaplanes was even more limited and these Albatros types made only a modest impact on the air war.

Bibliography

Books
Gray, Peter, and Thetford, Owen, *German Aircraft of the First World War*, second revised edition, New York: Doubleday & Company, Inc., 1970.

Grosz, Peter M., *Albatros W4*, Berkhamsted, Albatros Publications, 1995.

Herris, Jack, *Development of German Warplanes in WWI*, Aeronaut Books, 2012.

Herris, Jack, *German Armored Warplanes of WWI*, Aeronaut Books, 2012.

Lamberton, W.M., *Reconnaissance & Bomber Aircraft of the 1914–1918 War*, Letchworth, England, Harleyford Publications, 1962.

Nowarra, Heinz J., *Marine Aircraft of the 1914–1918 War*, Letchworth, Harleyford Publications Limited, 1966.

Ries, K. Recherchen zur Deutschen Luftfahrzeugrolle, Teil 1, 1919–1934, Diete Hoffmann, Mainz, 1977.

Z.A.K.(Zentral Abnahme Kommission, translated by Roland Jahn), *Geschichte der Deutschen Flugzeugindustrie*, Reichsdruckerie, 1918.

Articles
Gröschel, Dieter H.M., and Grosz, Peter M., Karriere und Misere des Dipl.-Ing. Otto Wiener von den Albatroswerken, *Propellerblatt Nr.27*, 2010.

Herris, Jack, "Rare Birds: Albatros J.II" *Over the Front* Vol.23 No.3, Autumn 2008.

Herris, Jack, "Rare Birds: Albatros C.IX & C.XIII" *Over the Front* Vol.27 No.1, Spring 2012.

Ott, G. "Zulassung und Kennzeichnung der deutschen Zivilflugzeuge 1914–1945" Pt.3. Luftfahrt international, 8/80/342.

Owers, Colin, "Albatros C.XV", *Over the Front* Vol.30 No.3, Autumn 2015.

Schmeelke, Michael, "Rare Birds: Albatros J.I *Infanterieflugzeug*", *Over the Front* Vol.21 No.1, Spring 2006.

Index

Name	Page
Christiansen, Friedrich	140, 141
Grohmann, Karl	44
Madelung, George	46
Schulz, *Lt.z.See*	91, 92
Thelen, Robert	46
Umlauff, *Lt.*	9

Albatros J.I J.424/17, previously photographed in 1917 insignia in the markings of an unknown unit, was later seen in summer 1918 markings.

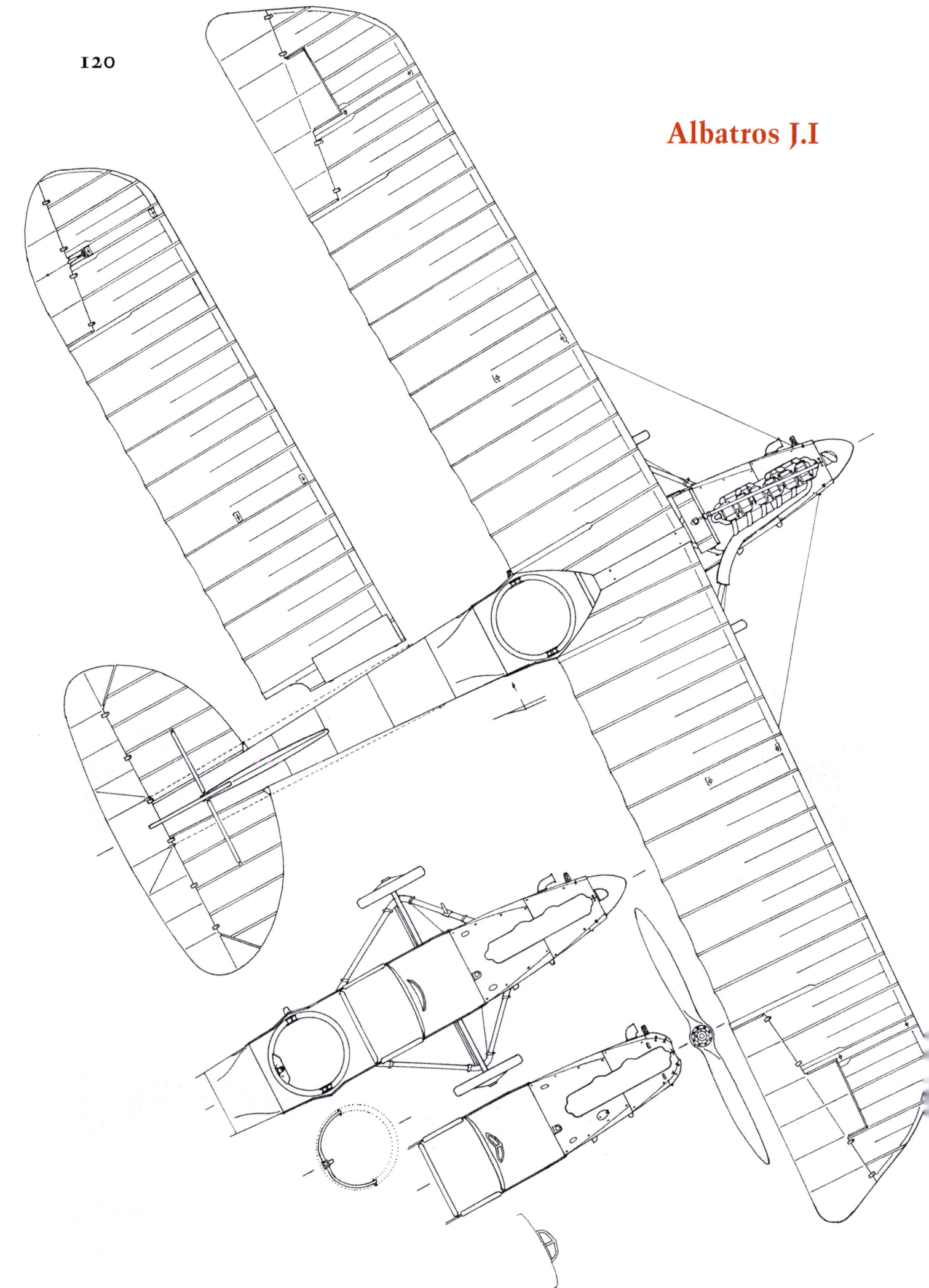
Albatros J.I

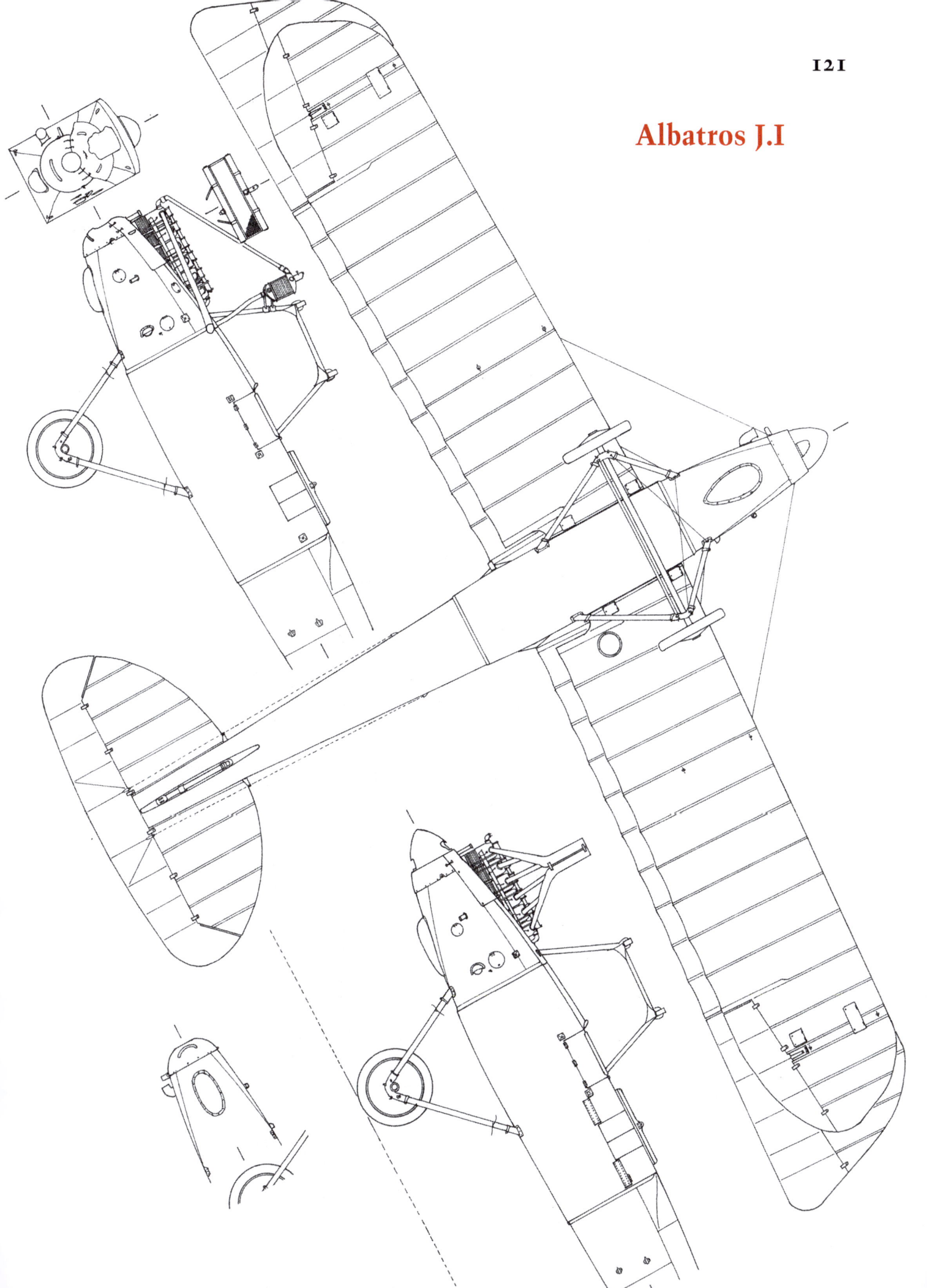
Albatros J.I

Albatros J.I

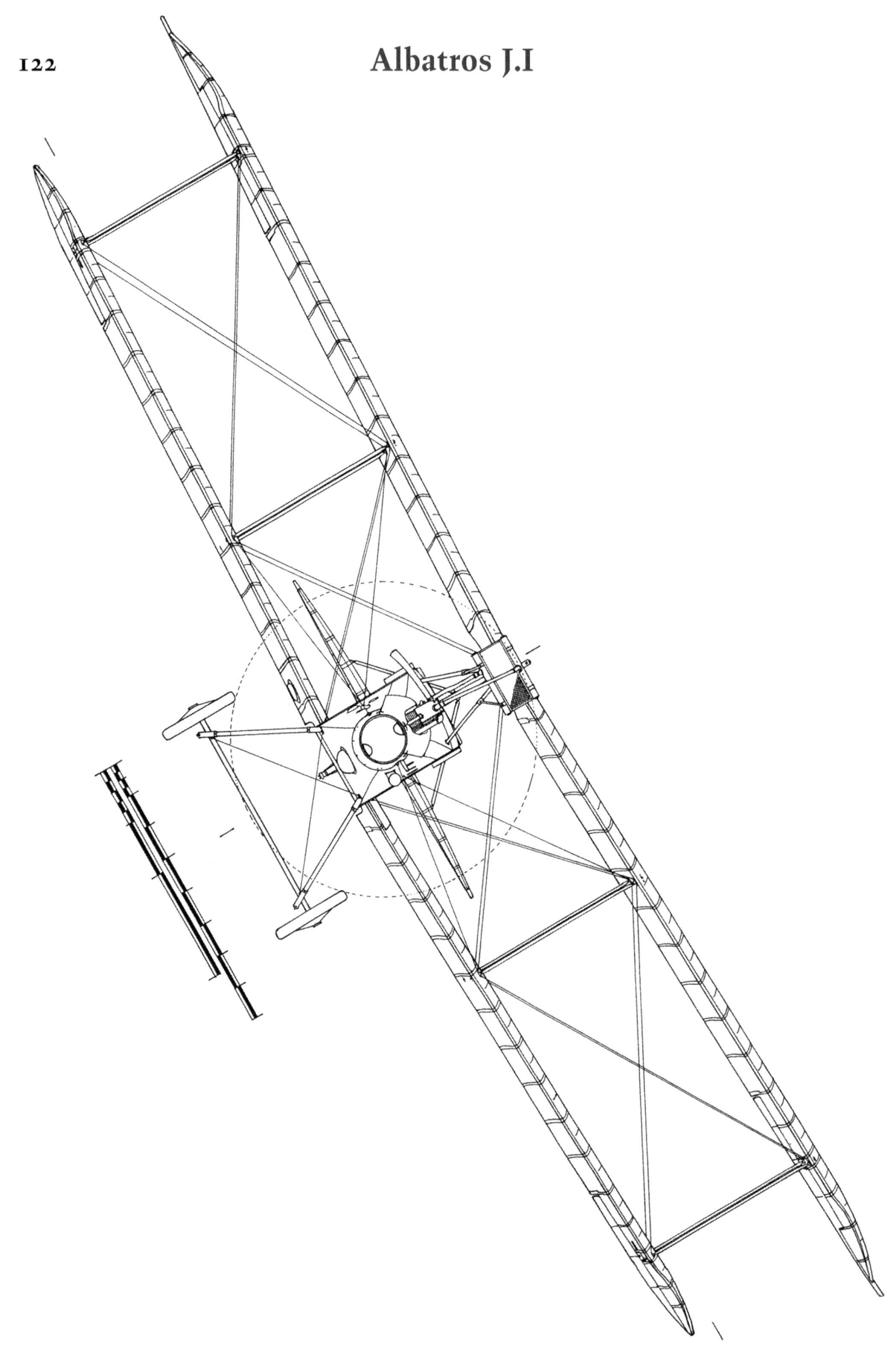

Albatros J.I

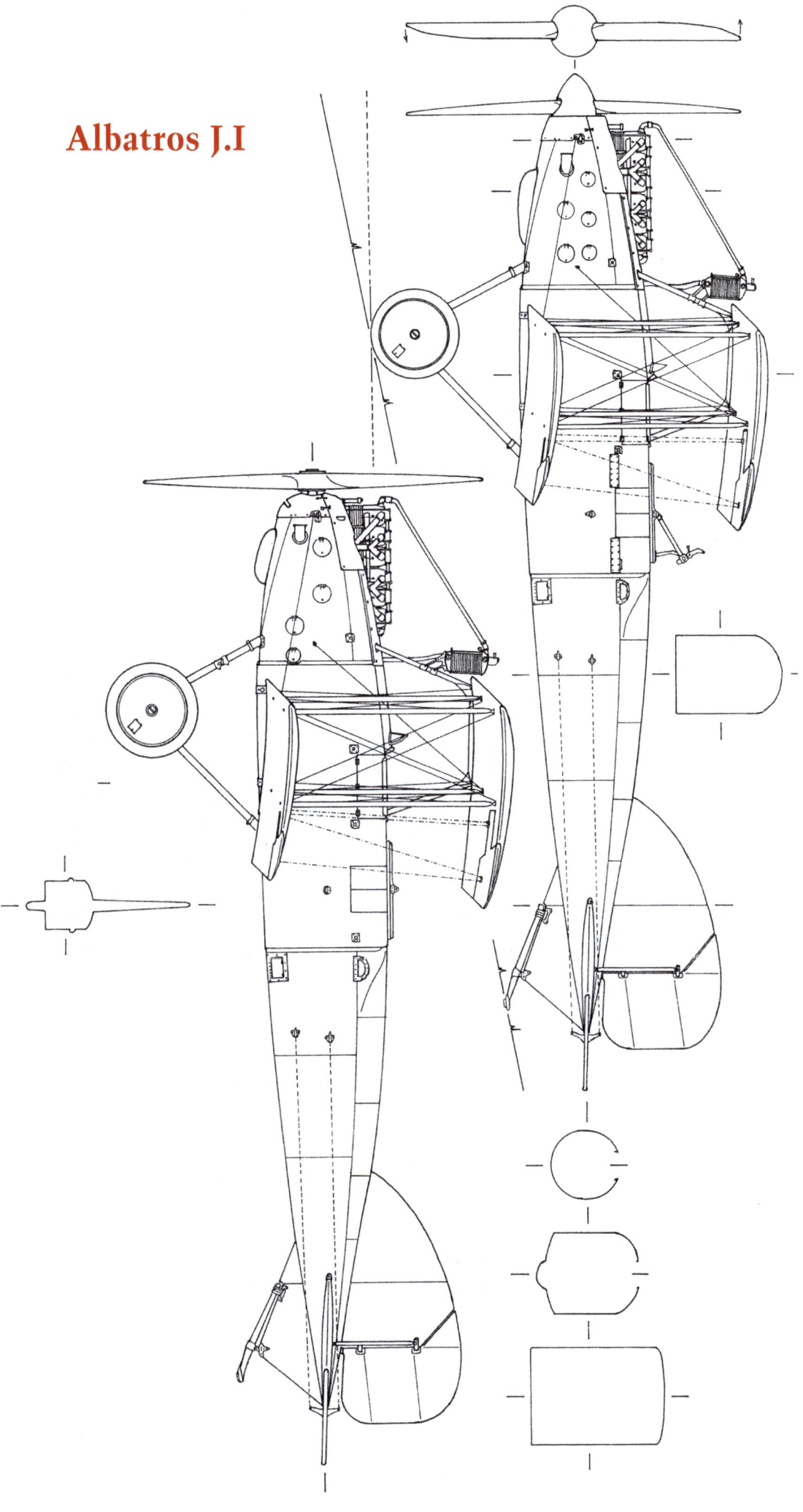

Albatros J.II

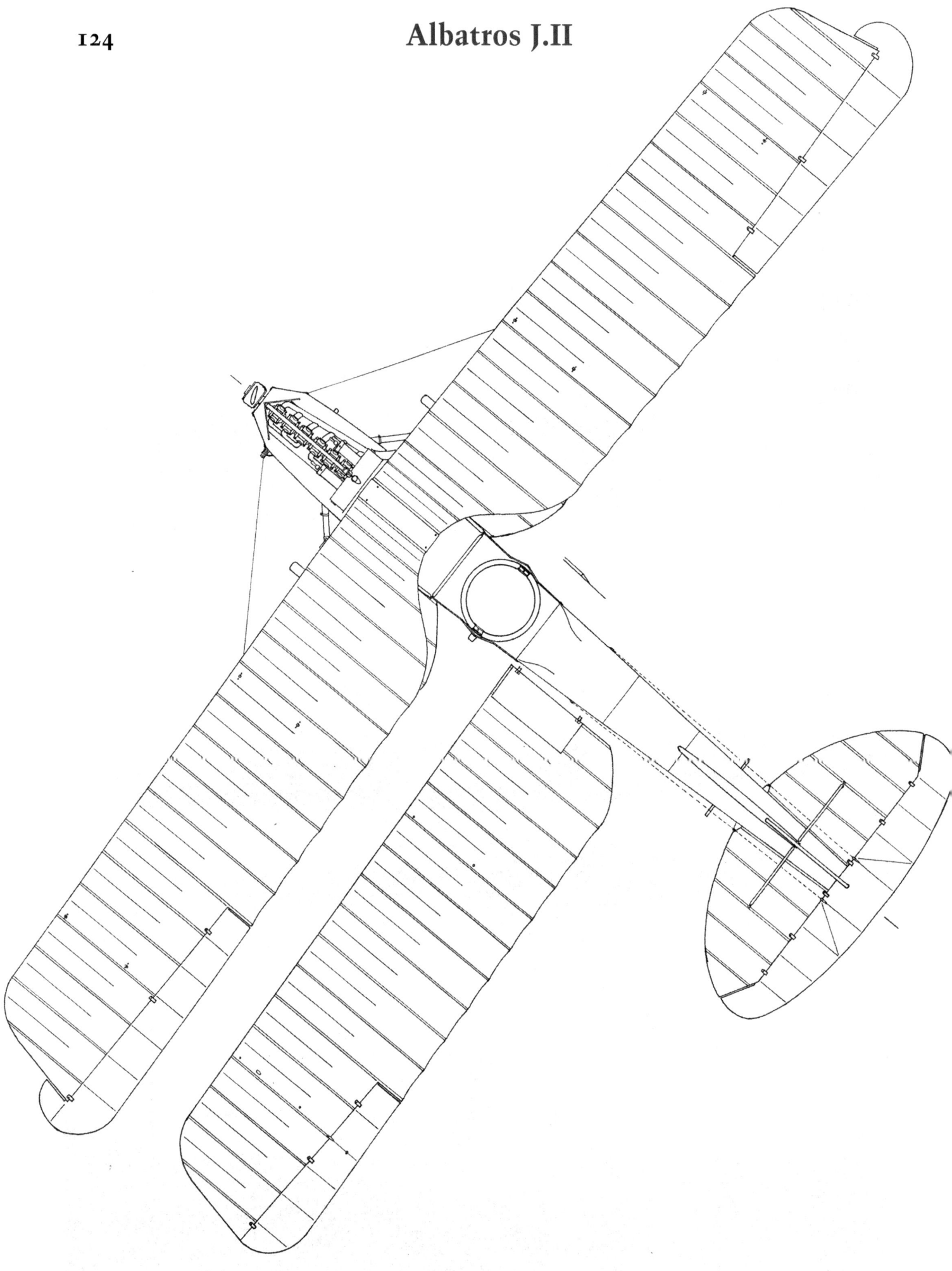

Albatros J.II

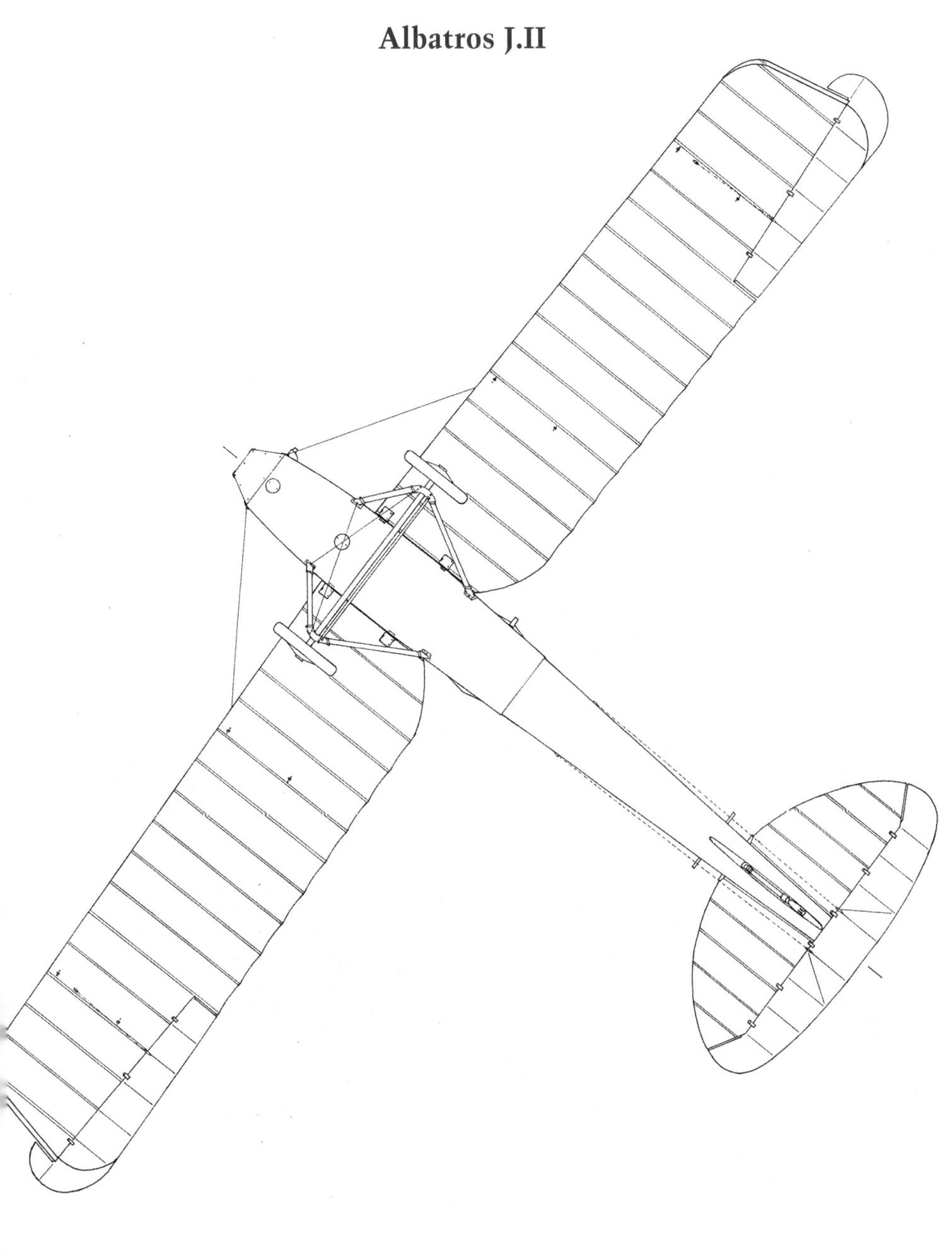

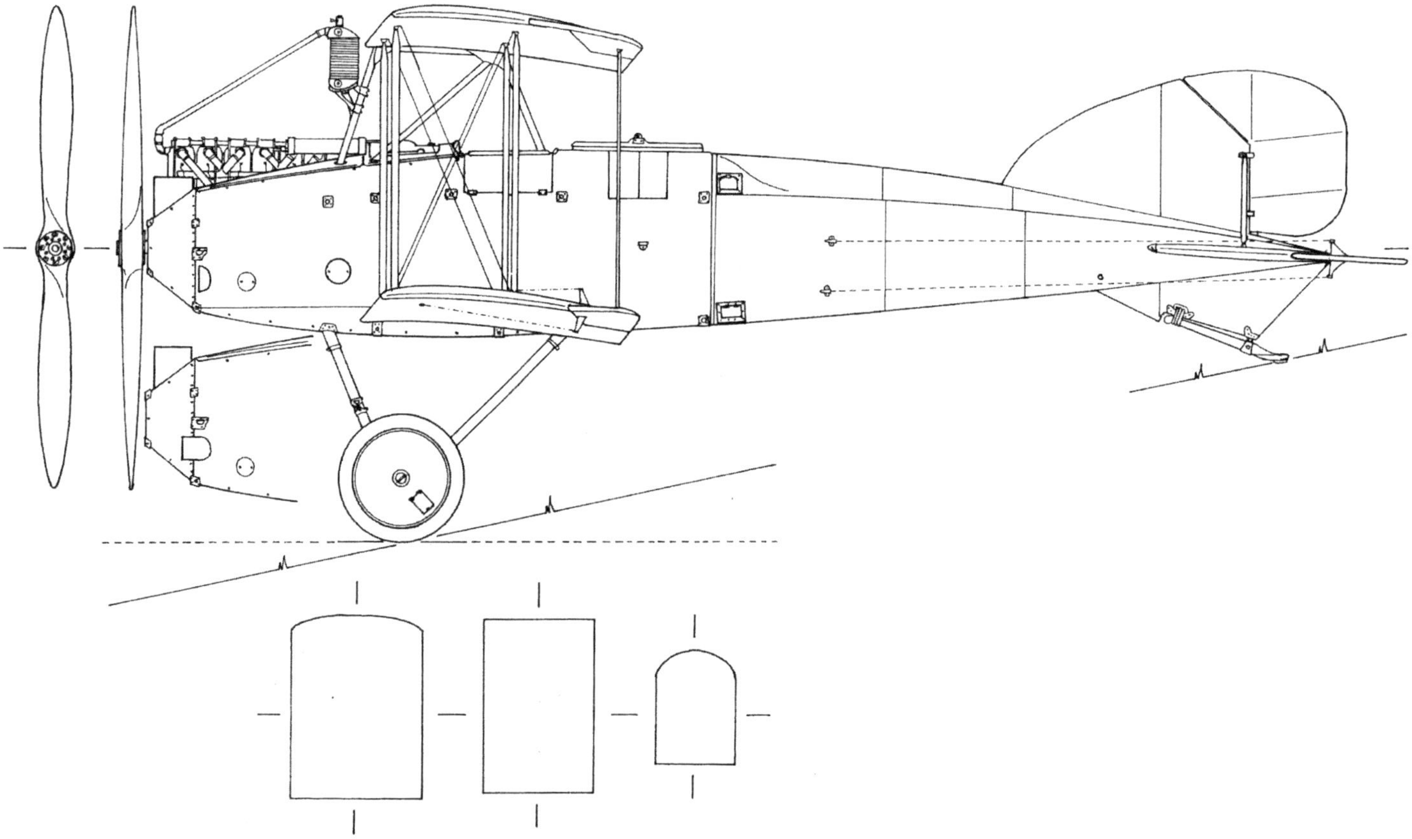

Albatros J.II

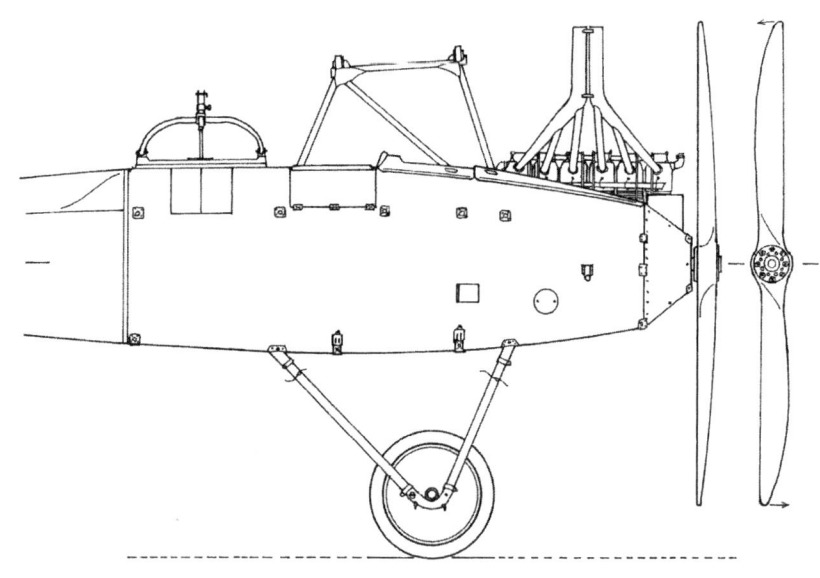

Albatros J.II

Albatros G.III

Albatros G.III

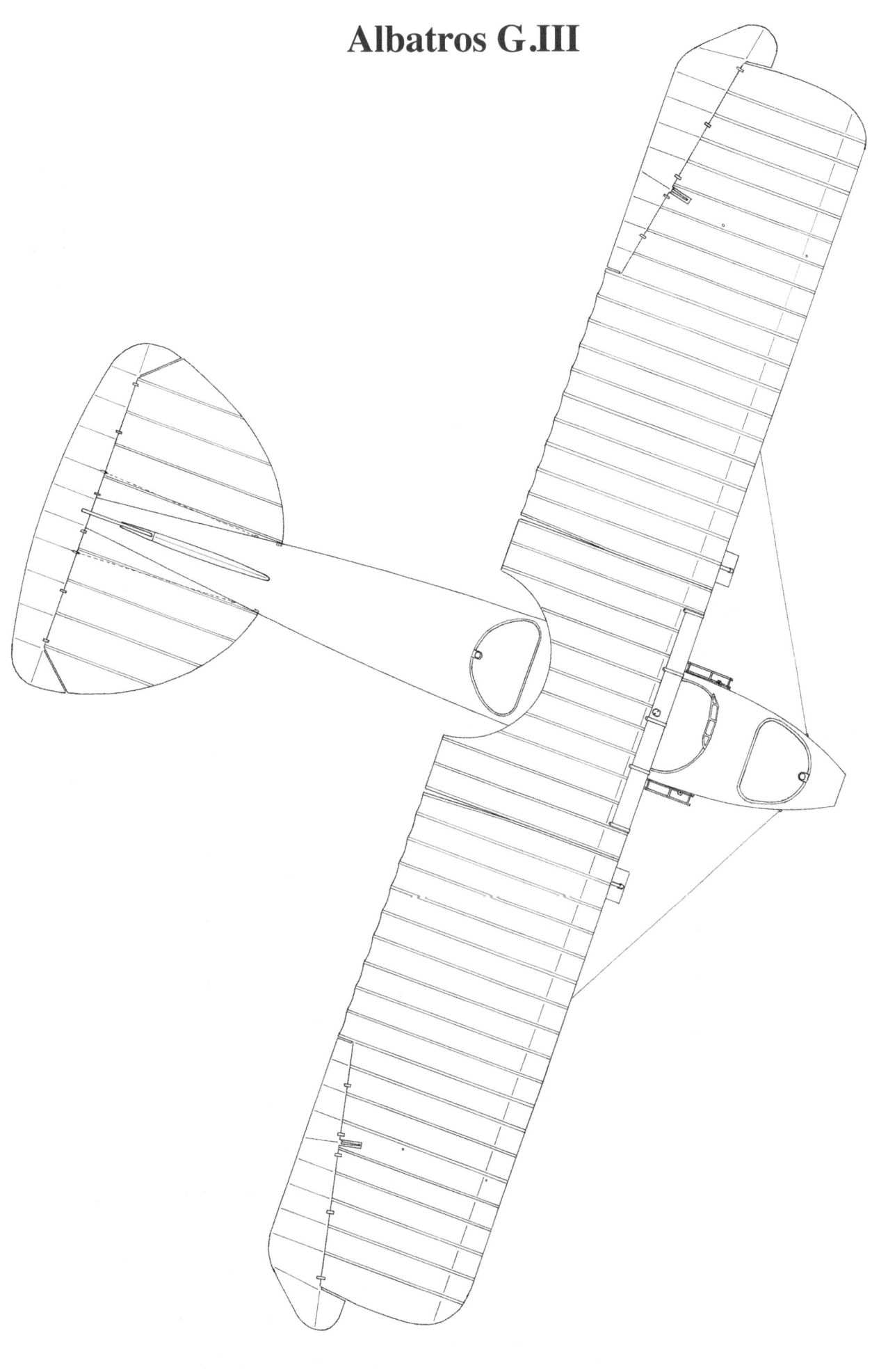

Albatros G.III

Albatros W.4 (Early)

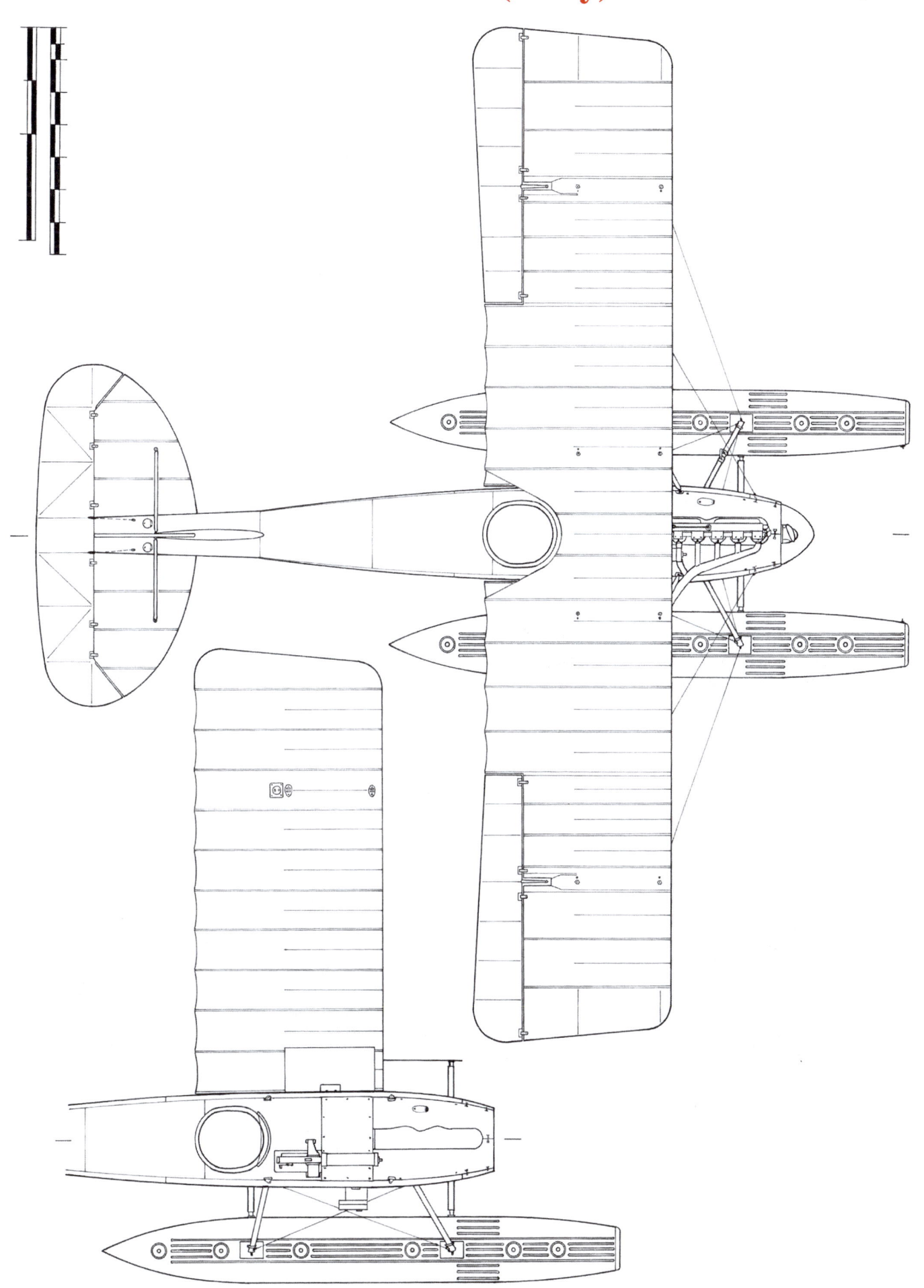

Albatros W.4 (Early)

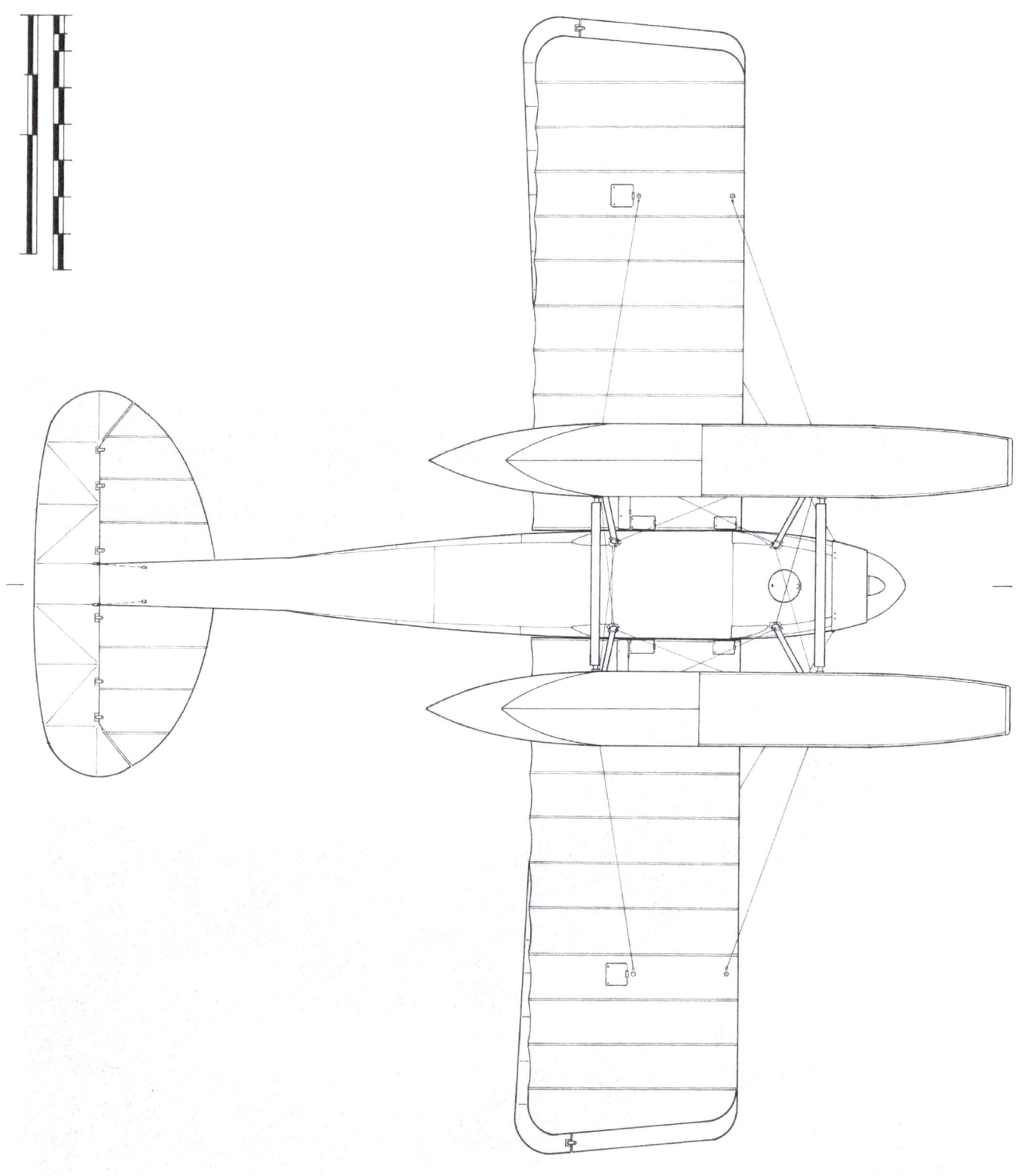

Albatros W.4 (Early)

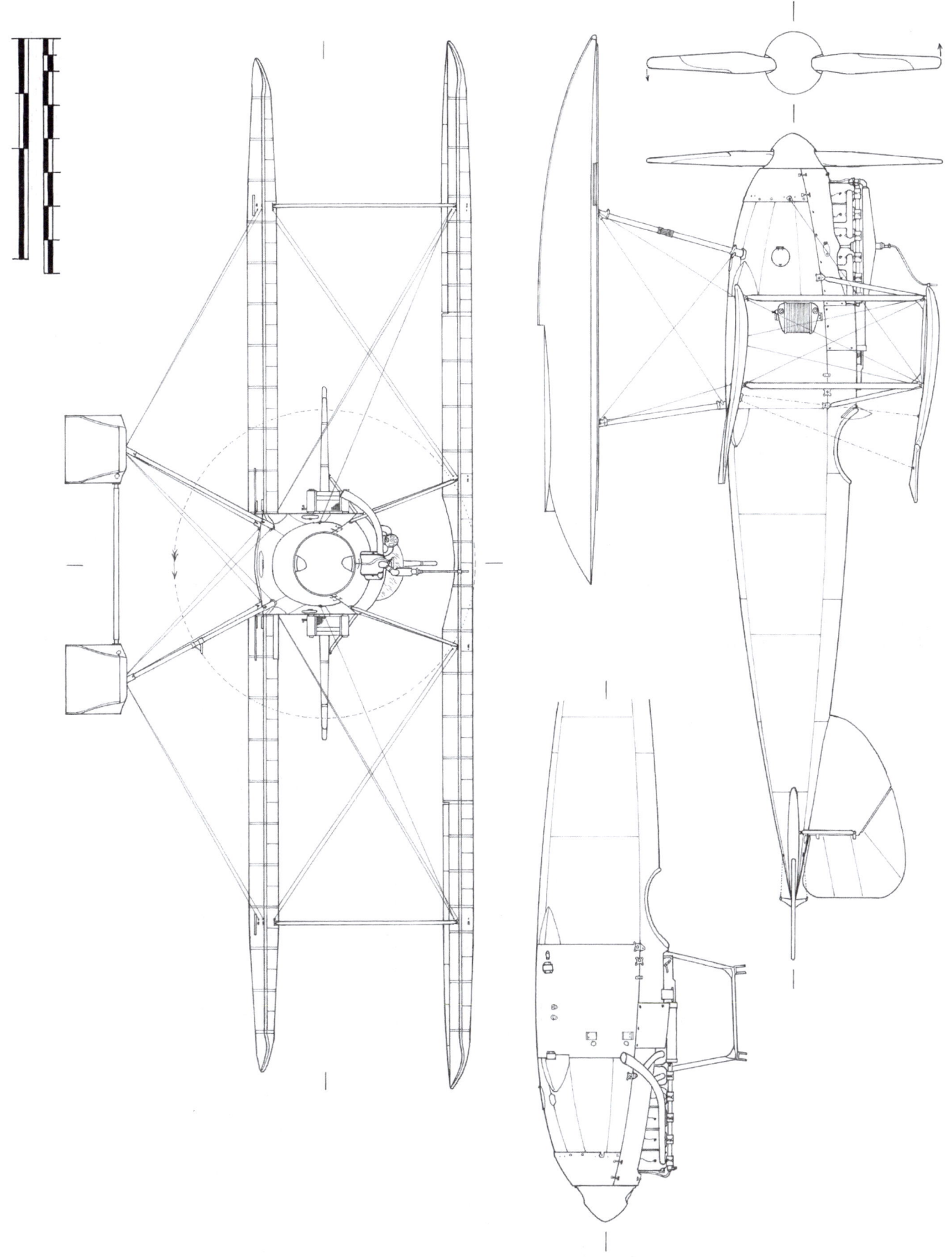

Albatros W.4 (Late)

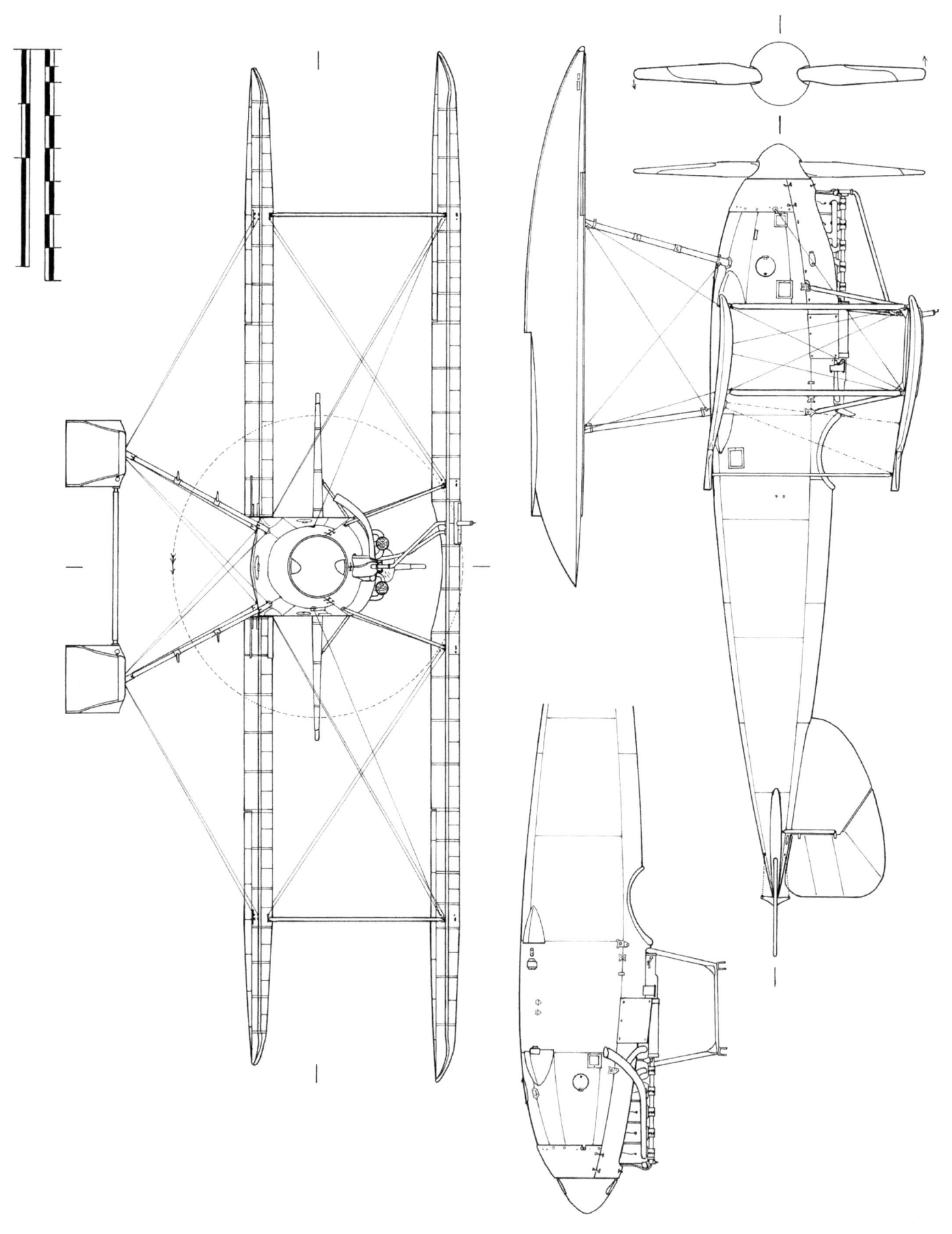

Albatros W.4 (Late)

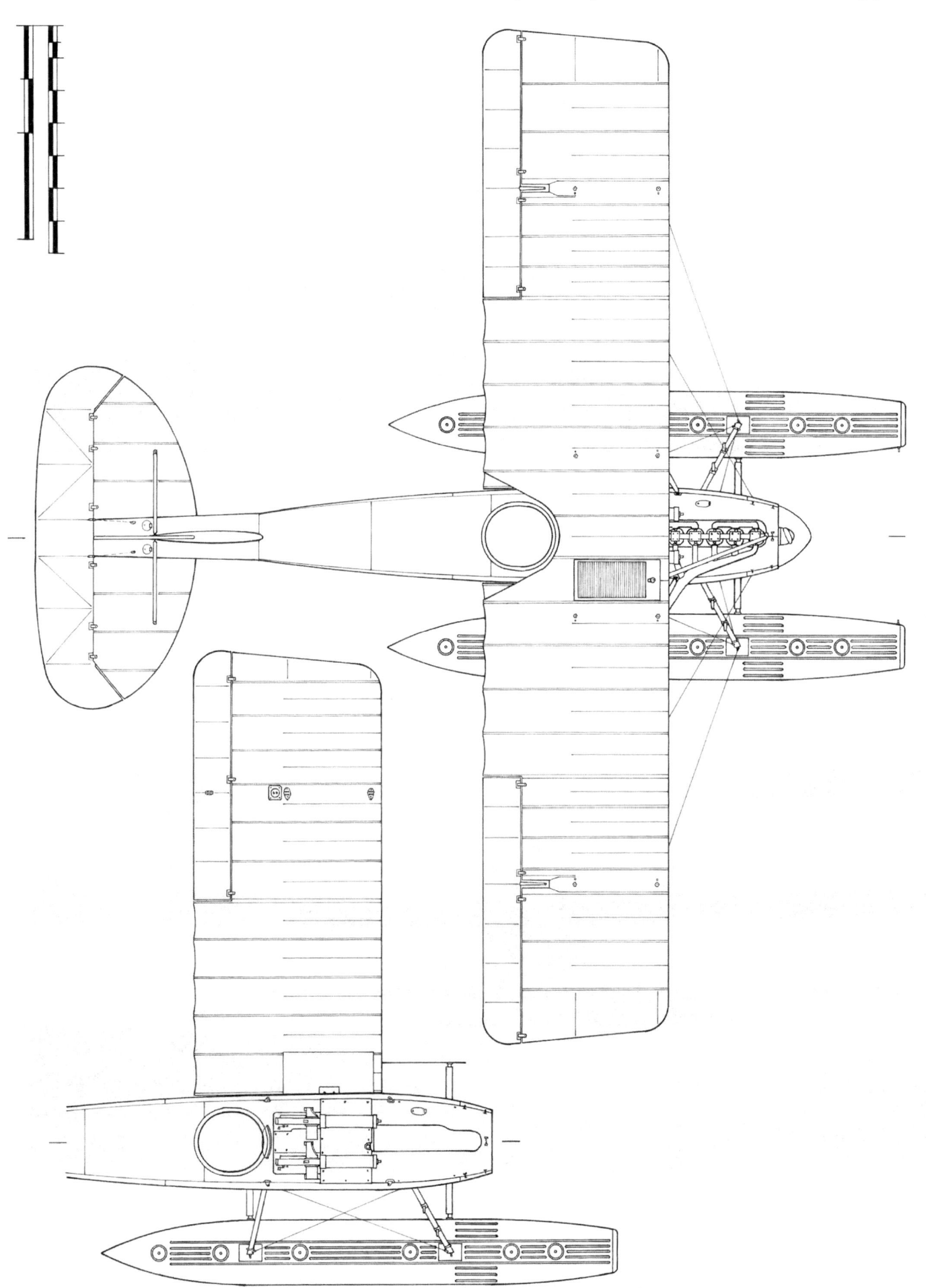

Albatros W.4 (Late)

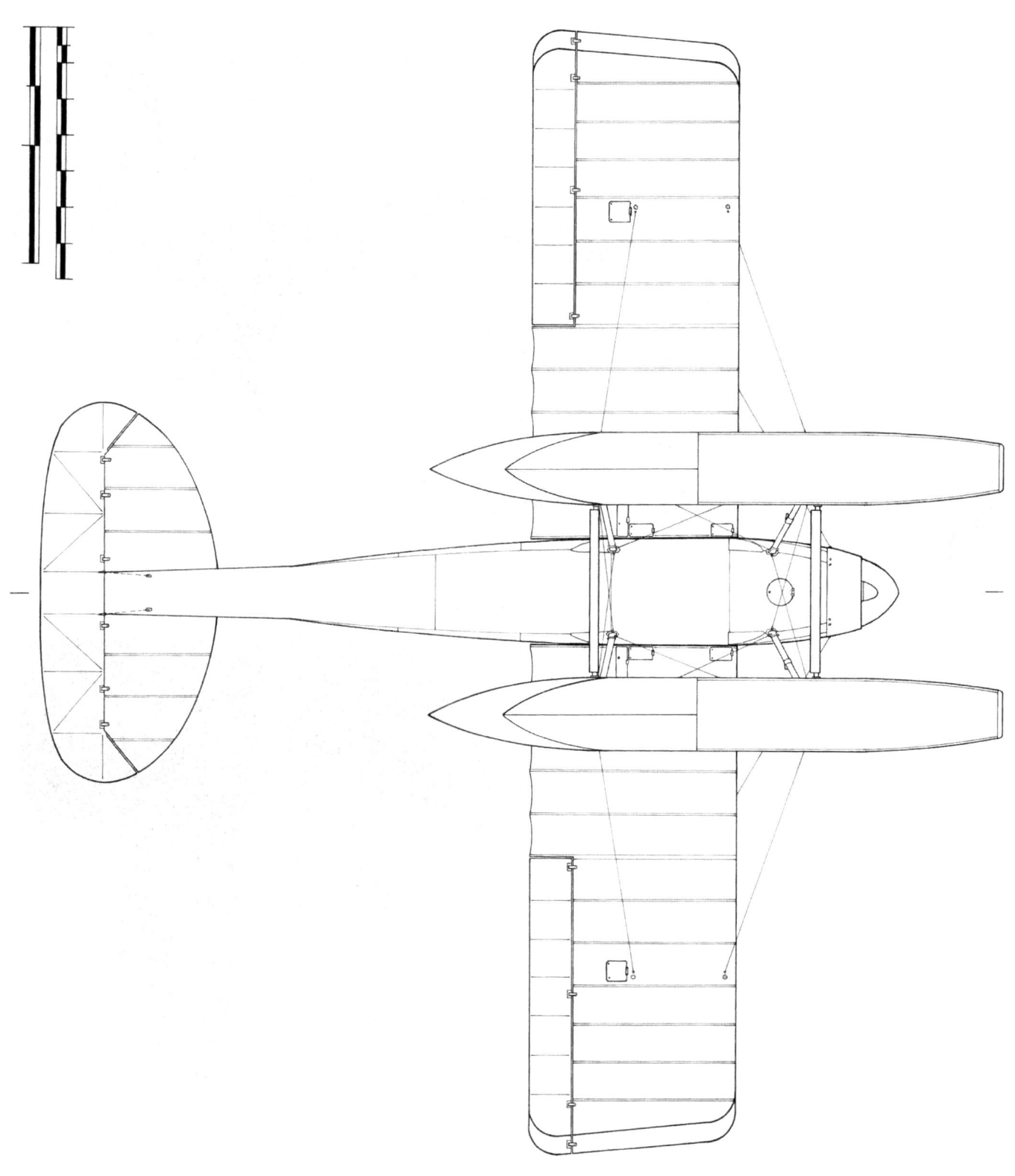

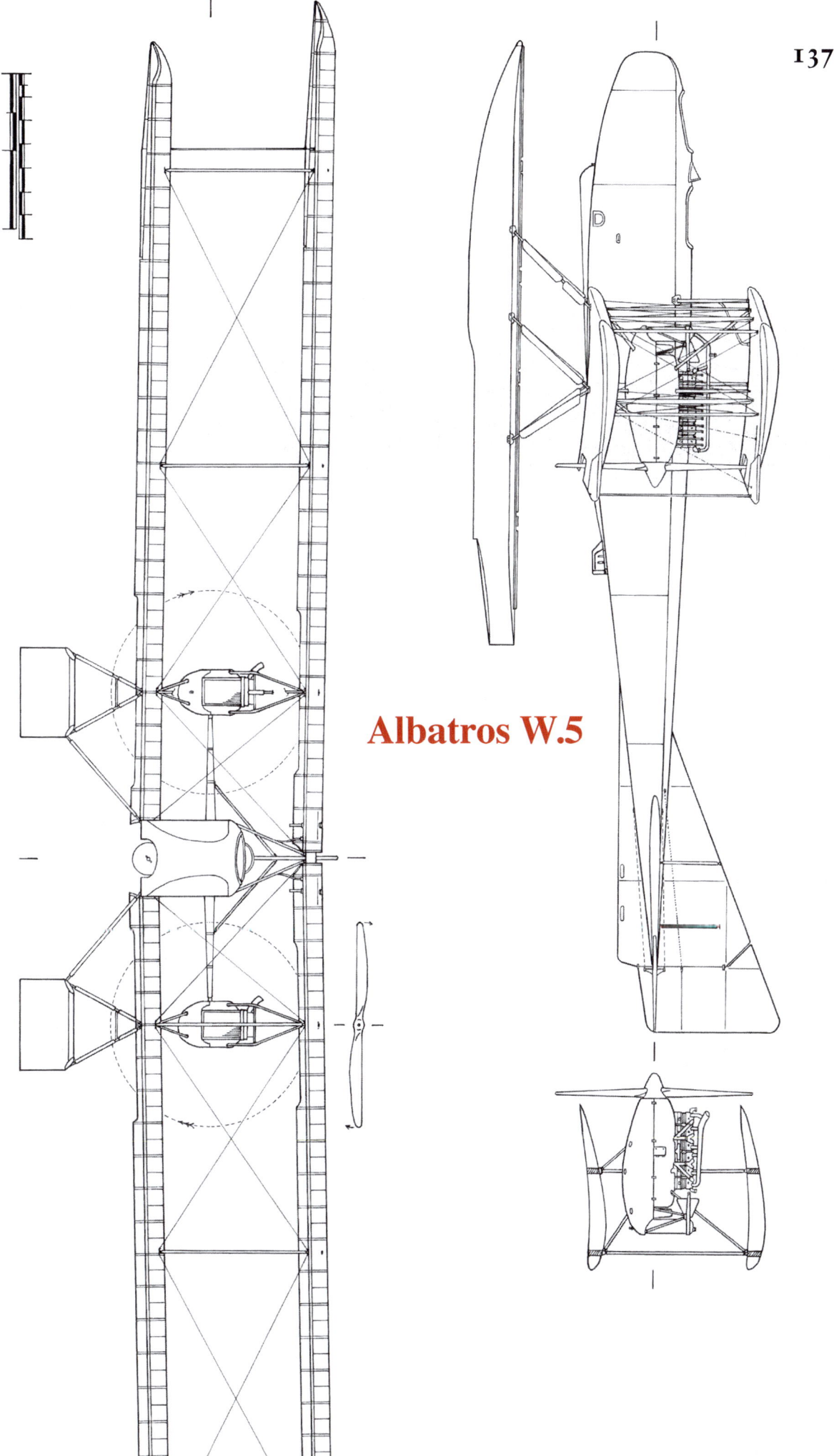
Albatros W.5

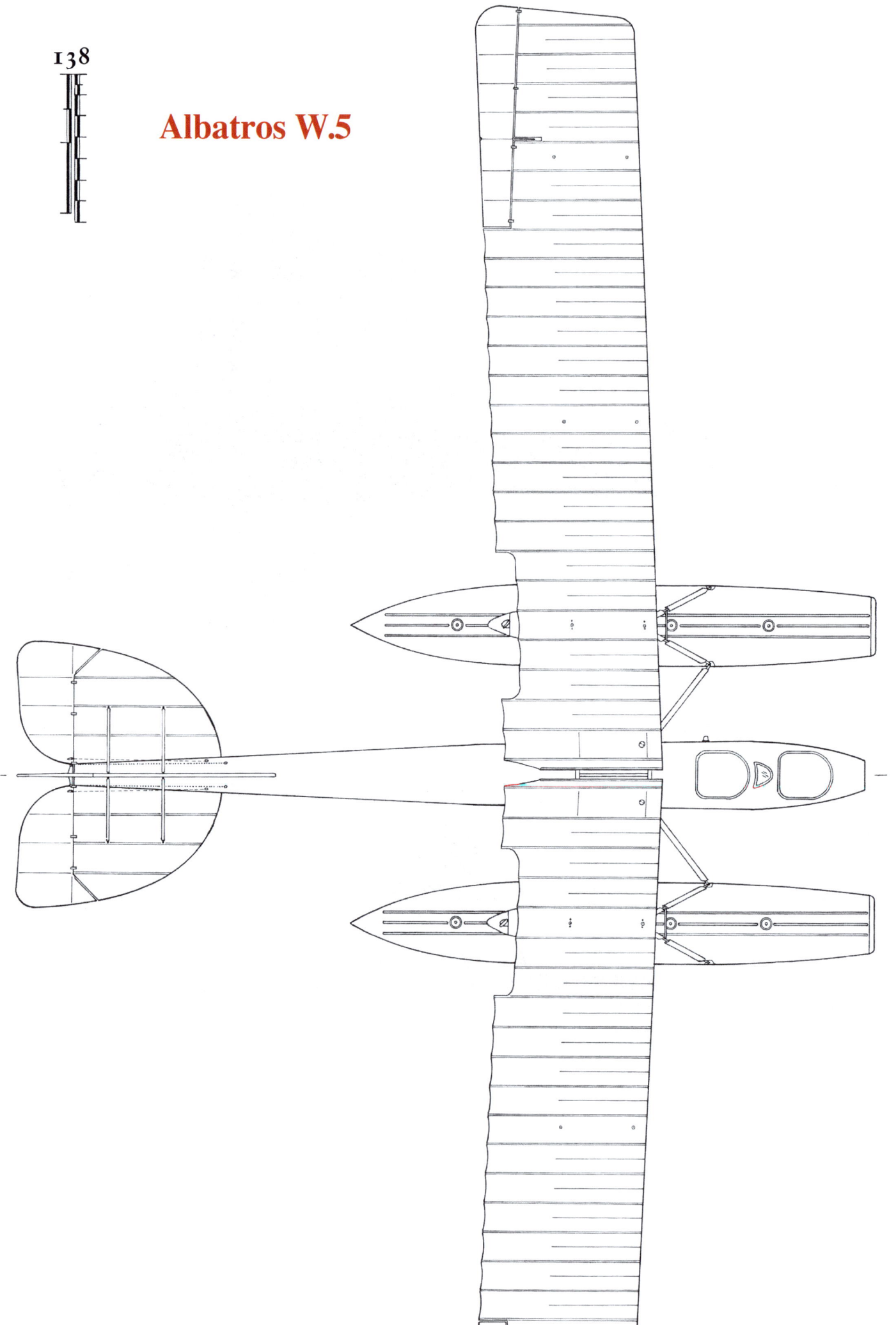
Albatros W.5

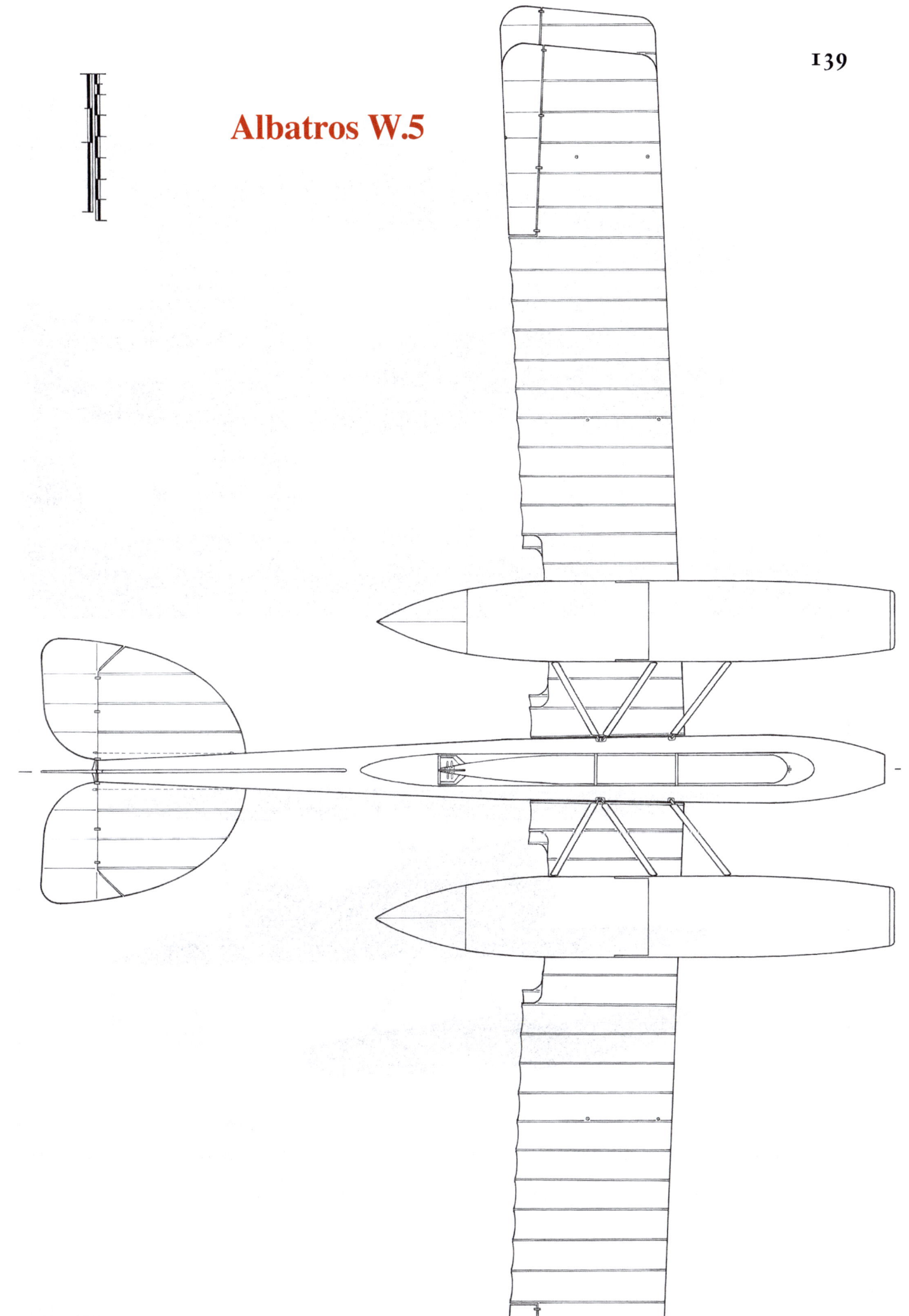

Afterword

Unfortunately, the aircrews flying Albatros armored J-types, bombers, and seaplanes and their operations remain little known and mostly anonymous. The exception is the most famous floatplane fighter ace and leader of them all, *Oblt.z.S.* Friedrich Christiansen. He is shown in a formal *Pour le Mérite* portrait at right, reproduced as Sanke card 609.

Christiansen served in the German merchant marine and volunteered for a year's service in the German navy in 1901. Deciding to fly, he got his pilot certificate in March 1914 and became a flight instructor. After the war started he was called back into military service as a naval aviator and was stationed at Zeebrugge on the English channel coast from 5 January 1915.

A very aggressive pilot, Christiansen flew numerous reconnaissance missions over the North Sea and even bombed Dover. When the Friedrichshafen FF33L two-seat floatplane fighter became available Christiansen flew it offensively, and he also flew the Albatros W.4 single-seat floatplane fighter. He scored his first air-to-air victory on 15 May 1917. In September 1917 he took command of *Seeflugstation Zeebrugge*, and scored his second victory on 1 October when flying the new Brandenburg W.12. Christiansen is credited with at least 13 victories, including airship *C27*, submarine *C25* (which survived damaged), eight twin-engine flying boats, a Sopwith Pup, and two Short 184 floatplanes. He also set the Dutch schooner *Meeuw* on fire on 21 April, 1918.

Surviving the war, Christiansen flew the 12-engine Do.X across the Atlantic in 1930, and later joined the German aviation ministry. He died 5 December 1972.

Above: *Oblt.z.S.* Friedrich Christiansen was the leading German seaplane ace. This formal portrait was taken after he was awarded the *Pour le Mérite*.

Albatros W.4 Marine #747 was given a splotchy camouflage pattern (exact pattern and colors unknown) and named *Möwe* (*Seagull*) after assignment to *Seeflugstation* Zeebrugge. It was flown by *Oblt.z.S.* Friedrich Christiansen.

Above: *Oblt.zur See* Friedrich Christiansen in the W.4 prototype, MN 747, at Zeebrugge. Now operational, this aircraft has had the fuselage cross modified by over-painting and was christened with the name *Möwe (Seagull)*.

Above: *Oblt.zur See* Friedrich Christiansen flying an Albatros W.4. Different float designs are evident in these W.4 photos; many different designs were tried to offer the best combination of handling on the water and in the air while maintaining water-tight integrity in the rough waters. Floats frequently needed replacement on operational aircraft. Christiansen scored 13 victories and was awarded the *Pour le Mérite*.

Albatros W.1

Albatros W.1 Marine Number 52. WWDs 52–56 were retroactively designated W.1s and their Marine Numbers given a '5' prefix to deceive Allied intelligence. Design of the tail surfaces and floats of the WDD/W.1 were in constant evolution.

Albatros W.1 Marine Number 226.

Albatros W.1 Marine Number 228.

Printed in Great Britain
by Amazon